Teaching:
Sign Language for the
Early Childhood
Environment

By: Dr. Michael & Lillian Hubler

Teaching: Sign Language for the Early Childhood Environment

TABLE OF CONTENTS

INTRODUCTION

From the moment of birth, infants are ready to learn and capable of processing information from the world around them. In addition, research has shown that young children, who develop in a healthy social and emotional environment, also learn better academically.

Teaching American Sign Language (ASL) to hearing children has become increasingly widespread in early childhood toddler and preschool curricula. By using sign language as a tool to enhance overall communication, our hearing children grow in the four major early childhood domains of social-emotional learning, language development, cognitive and perceptual growth, and fine and gross motor development.

Teaching sign language to young children promotes early communication and school readiness by building characteristics such as: confidence, curiosity, self-control, cooperation, and empathy. These skills are vital to the overall development of children as they help them to better manage the responsibilities of home and school.

The visual nature of signing has a positive impact on relationship building as well. Many parents have observed that they have more affectionate relationships with their signing children because the parents understand what their child needs and are able to meet those needs immediately.

This book provides songs, games, stories, crafts, and other activities to which American Sign Language (ASL) can be easily incorporated. Learning sign language is easy and fun. This lesson planning instruction guide will enable you to teach infants, toddlers, preschoolers and school age children basic sign language in a simple, fun, educational manner—but don't stop there. Keep signing with your young children as they grow and begin elementary school in order to maximize the communication, social-emotional, and academic benefits.

Time to Sign, Inc. is the foremost expert on the instruction of sign language for parents and teachers of young children. All our materials and trainings have been uniquely designed by our panel of experts which include: early childhood educators, communication specialists, special needs childhood educators, deaf and hard of hearing professionals, college professors, audiologists, speech pathologists, and ASL specialists.

Text Book Description

This book is designed to give educational programs a variety of tools to use in the classroom to teach American Sign Language (ASL). The book includes theory and research on the benefits of signing with children. Content on ASL background, other forms of manual communication, language development milestones, age appropriate signs and activities, using sign language for classroom and behavior management, and working with special needs. Additional content includes over 300 signs plus handouts with signs, songs, games and activities.

Objectives

At the end of this course, the successful learner should b e able to:

1. Identify and explain influencing factors of the benefits of using sign language.
2. Discuss the differences in the forms of communication.
3. Describe how to incorporate sign language into classroom routines while keying in on developmental milestones.
4. Become familiar with sign language topical sets included in the text.
5. Learn strategies and signs for classroom behavior management and smooth transitions.
6. Learn how to incorporate signs to augment learning with special needs children.

CHAPTER 1: SIGNING WITH YOUNG CHILDREN INFORMATION & BENEFITS

When Should I Start Signing With My Child?

You can begin signing with your children at any time, but the sooner the better for achieving the maximum benefits. Signing with your child from birth is becoming increasingly common. Start with some key basic signs to meet children's wants and needs. Children are perpetually "in the moment". For learning to occur, it must be connected or associated to a current event.

For example, just prior to offering more milk (bottle or nursing), use the signs "more" and "milk." Repeated, consistent use of a sign in context will allow children to begin making the connection on their own. They will try to imitate the sign themselves. Eventually, you will even see you child respond to your signs for "more milk" with a yes or no movement.

Also, to continue to receive the many benefits of sign language for enhanced social, emotional, and academic learning it is suggested that you continue the use of sign language throughout their early childhood education and into elementary school.

Benefits of Sign Language for Young Children

1. Learning to understand the expression of emotions and facial expressions helps children learn to communicate their feelings in a positive way.
2. By expanding vocabulary, social opportunities, and opportunities for success in learning, sign language enhances self-esteem and promotes self-control.
3. When children are emotionally comforted they gain confidence and build self-esteem.
4. Children develop better communication skills through sign language; which in turn makes them more independent, enables play through enhanced social capabilities, and subsequently makes them happier. They are better able to have fun with their friends by reducing conflict and/or stressful situations by better understanding, expressing, and reacting positively to the emotions of others.
5. Sign language is a pictorial representation of the word or concept; as such parents, caregivers, and teachers can understand and respond more quickly to their children's needs. Meeting a young child's needs immediately reduces their frustration; which in turn promotes positive behavior and interactions with others around them.
6. Sign language is a great way for infant and toddlers to communicate their wants and needs before their vocal cords have developed to be able to say the word.
7. Sign language accelerates the acquisition of speech by stimulating areas of the brain that are associated with speech and language. Using spoken vocabulary with signing will enhance language development.
8. Signing provides language stimulation and conceptual information that enhances vocabulary development in children.
9. Sign language is a two-sided brain activity whereas hearing is not. Signing actually causes more synapses to "fire up", in essence building the brain. Sign language has been shown to boost IQ's between 8 and 13 points per child, for every child that uses it at an early age for a prolonged period of time.
10. Sign language as a second language readies the brain for additional language learning.

11.   Sign language is easier to learn than the spoken word. This enables success in language acquisition by teaching children to understand more words and concepts at an earlier age. It also builds success as even children with speech/communication delays can learn and do signs to communicate their wants and needs. When comparing a "normal" hearing child with a child of deaf adults (CODA), the CODA child will be taught and learn 100 more concepts on average than the "normal" hearing child.

12.   Using both sign language and speech together can speed the learning process, as it adds redundancy, which facilitates quicker and better recall of words and concepts.

13.   Approximately 80% of signs are iconic or pictorial representations of what the sign represents. As such, signs are easier to learn than the spoken word. This also greatly benefits the visual, tactile, or kinesthetic learner.

14.   Sign language enhances the development of pre and early literacy skills. Children using sign language are more successful in math concepts and alphabet knowledge.

15.   Using many modes of input strengthens connections in the brain and therefore helps children to retain information longer because it supplements speech reception, recall, and ability.

Classroom Benefits of Signing with Young Children

1. Lowers children's noise levels in the classroom.

2. Reduces need for teachers to raise their voice.

3. Enables class to support special needs children.

4. Children pay better attention; they have to look directly at you.

5. Sign language gets their attention better than the spoken word.

6. Increased ability to express themselves reduces instances of misbehavior.

7. Provides children the ability to positively express their emotions.

8. Increases children's use of manners.

Helpful Information About Signing

- Dominant Hand: Use your dominant hand to begin all your signs.

- Reference Hand: Your reference hand is your non-dominant hand. Your reference hand is used to support your dominant hand when two hands are needed to create the sign. Usually the reference hand is the non-movement hand or non-active hand. Although, some individuals do indeed sign with just one hand.

- Negative and Positive Modifier: Shake your head to "no" or "yes" as you produce the sign. For example, shake your head "no" and then do the sign for touch for instructions to not touch.

- Facial Expression: Use your facial expressions as part of your sign. When doing command signs you must look strict with your facial expression. When asking a question your eyebrow area should look like you are puzzled.

- Nose up and Nose Down (Male and Female): From your nose up is for male signs, specifically when doing signs for male signs such as Dad, Brother, Grandfather, Boy, Nephew, and Uncle. From nose down is for female signs such as Mother, Grandmother, Girl, Nieces, and Aunt. In between denotes Nieces and Nephews, or both sexes.

- Signing Window: Keep all signs in a frame from the head to the middle of the chest area.

- Movement Signs: You should move when you do animal signs. Also, all action signs move once. For example, the sign for eat is to move your dominant hand to your mouth once, while holding it there without movement denotes food.

- Facial Expressions – should support what you are signing. "Your face will surely show it."

- I Love You Sign – combines the letters I, L, and Y.

- Person Indicator – "er". Both hands just inside the shoulder, palms facing each other, hands coming down simultaneously from the shoulders to the waist.

Tips for Teachers/Parents/Caregivers

Be Patient
Start with one word at a time. Children may understand when you sign and respond, but it is okay if it takes a child more time to sign it themselves. Use the sign word and the spoken word together. A wall is built brick by brick; likewise communication is built word by word.

Be Consistent
Use the same word frequently, in context, so that the correct meaning is attached to that word. For example, sign 'drink' whenever the child is drinking, when you give them a drink or they see someone else drinking. Doing the same thing at the same time is how routines are built. Routines can provide structure and order to your child's day.

Be Positive
Your child may also approximate the sign word long before being able to get the hand shape right. Give genuine praise for every effort, but keep teaching the correct sign. Gently shape their hand to reflect the correct sign. Everyone learns better in an environment of encouragement. Shower your child with praise for their effort. This builds his/her self-esteem and confidence to try more.

Have Fun
This book contains lesson plans for young children, infant through kindergarten, which will enhance their communication. Use these stories, games, songs, and activities with sign language to make your children's learning fun.

Thank you for giving the gift of sign language to your children!

CHAPTER 2: EARLY CHILDHOOD SOCIAL & EMOTIONAL PATTERNS OF DEVELOPMENT

Social, Emotional, and Academic Learning (SEAL)

Currently, only 40% of children starting kindergarten are rated by their teachers as being socially and emotionally ready for elementary school. This greatly impacts their behavior and academic success. Sign language also can be used to facilitate this social and emotional learning, as well as to increase their peer relations and communications skills. Together these skills help to set the needed trajectory to prepare children for scholastic and life success. Teachers who sign with their children in the classroom report that it helps with their social and emotional development, enhancing classroom behavior, and resulting school readiness.

Understanding children's social and emotional communication languages helps to reinforcing the use of their natural gifts and abilities to support their social and emotional learning; which in turn provides for enhanced academic learning. Sign language also can be used to facilitate this social and emotional learning, as well as to increase their peer relations and communications skills. Together these skills help to set the needed trajectory to prepare children for scholastic and life success.

Specifically, teachers find sign language extremely useful in teaching children to understand and use manners, to express their emotions in a positive manner, as well as in the general day to day management of their classrooms. Sign language also enhances young children's communication skills, concept understanding, and broadens their vocabulary; which helps enhance their social skills and interactions with peers and teachers.

Social & Emotional Development
Learning & Development Standards - Birth to Four

Sign Language Use as it Correlates to the Standards:

Words = Signs/Actions/Communication/Gestures

Sign language encourages the development in the following skills and may promote the skill development at a earlier age then children not using sign.

Development Benchmarks
Birth to Eight Months

Self Regulation

1. Develops early behavioral regulation

2. Develops early emotional regulation

3. Develops early social problem-solving

Self-Concept

1. Becomes aware of oneself as a unique individual while still connected to others

2. Demonstrates emerging sense of competence and confidence in growing abilities

3. Forms and maintains mutual relationships with others

Trust and Emotional Security

1. Experiences and develops secure relationships

2. Responds to the environment

Developmental Benchmarks
8-18 Months

Self Regulation

1. Demonstrates developing behavior regulation
2. Demonstrates developing social problem-solving
3. Demonstrates developing emotional regulation

Self-Concept

1. Becomes aware of self as a unique individual while still connected to others.
2. Demonstrates increasing sense of competence and confidence in growing abilities
3. Forms and maintains mutual relationships with others

Trust and Emotional Security

1. Experiences and develops secure relationships
2. Responds to the environment

Developmental Benchmarks
18-24 Months – Toddlers

Self Regulation
1. Demonstrates increasing behavior regulation
2. Demonstrates increasing emotional regulation
3. Demonstrates increasing social problem- solving

Self-Concept

1. Becomes aware of self as a unique individual while still connected to others
2. Demonstrates increasing sense of competence and confidence in growing abilities
3. Forms and maintains mutual relationships with others

Trust and Emotional Security

1. Forms and maintains secure relationships with others

2. Responds to the environment

Developmental Benchmarks - Two Year Olds

Self Regulation

1. Demonstrates increasing behavior regulation

2. Demonstrates increasing emotional regulation

3. Demonstrates increasing social problem- solving

Self-Concept

1. Becomes aware of oneself as a unique individual while still connected to others

2. Demonstrates increasing sense of competence and confidence in growing abilities

3. Forms and maintains mutual relationships with others

Trust and Emotional Security

1. Forms and maintains secure relationships with others

2. Responds to the environment

Developmental Benchmarks - Three Year Olds
Pro-Social Behavior

1. Develops positive relationships and interacts comfortably with familiar adults

2. Interacts with and develops positive relationships with peers

3. Joins in group activities and experiences within early learning environments

4. Shows care and concern for others

Self Regulation

1. Adapts to transitions with support

2. Begins to use materials with increasing care and safety

3. Follows simple rules and familiar routines with support

4. Shows developing ability to solve social problems with support from familiar adults

Self-Concept

1. Begins to independently initiate and direct so experiences
2. Shows growing confidence in their abilities

Understanding and Using Our Four Brains
Early Childhood Education Strategies & Signs

Our Emotional & Creative Brain

Our Emotional Brain is located in the Right Brain area. This is the area of the brain that recognizes facial, emotional, musical, color, pictorial, intuition, and creative expressions. Research indicates that our young children spend almost **60%** of their time in the Emotional Brain. Our Emotional Brain is reactionary, meaning that logic usage associated with the left side of the brain is at our lowest when we use our emotional brain for decision making. Children tend to react immediately without thinking about the potential consequences of their action when they use this Right Brain area.

Our Logical Analytical Brain

Our Logical Brain is located within the left hemisphere. This is the area of the brain that recognizes spoken language, logic, critical thinking, analytical thinking, numbers, and reasoning. Research indicates that our young children spend only about **25%** of their time in the logical area. As children develop the use of their Logical Brain increases. Science tells us that using our Logical Brain helps us to self-regulate our emotions. Learning to use logic helps us solve problems, complete mathematical equations, deal effectively with peers, and more.

Our Heart Brain

The Heart Brain in many cultures is considered the source of emotions, passion, and wisdom. It is believed that people feel they experience the sensation of love and other emotional states in the area of the heart. Science has shown us that in fact the heart communicates with the Emotional Brain and significantly impacts how we perceive and react to the world.

Our Gut Brain

The Gut Brain is commonly referred to as our "second brain" and it influences both our behavior and well being. The Gut Brain is a mass of neural tissue, filled with important neurotransmitters that directly connect our Gut Brain to our Emotional Brain. The Gut Brain is equipped to work independently of the Emotional or Logical Brain. The Gut Brain also transmits information to our Emotional and Logical Brain by altering emotional moods and our reactions to stressful situations. Indeed, this is the reason we are told that children cannot learn when they are hungry, as the Gut Brain overrides all critical thinking and learning and nothing else matters but meeting the base need of getting food.

Early Childhood Social and Emotional Patterns

The Speaker
Patterns: The speaker loves to talk to and encourage others, and learns through communication.

Maximizing Learning: Dedicate time to listening to them, have them communicate class instructions to others, pair them with shy children, and allow them to verbally participate in circle time and other activities.

speak   person

help   person

The Helper
Patterns: The helper loves to help and serve others.

Maximizing Learning: Have them assist with setup, cleanup, and leading of activities; have them buddy with new, shy, or special needs students; have them run errands in class; and give them verbal and visual praise daily.

The Time Keeper
Patterns: The time keeper loves spending time in the company of others, and wants to know when things will happen.

Maximizing Learning: Have them participate in group activities, give them individual attention to reinforce their learning and behavior, put them in charge of the activity clock, take walks as a group, and give the gift of yourself, your time.

value   time   person

gift   person

The Gifter
Patterns: The gifter loves to make and bring things to others.
Maximizing Learning: Have them make daily art projects to take home to family, give verbal praise daily, give them thoughtful personalized gifts, and give the gift of your presence.

The Hugger
Patterns: The hugger loves to give and receive affection, and engage in physical touch (hug, pat on the back, high fives, etc.).
Maximizing Learning: Greet and say goodbye daily with a positive touches, hug, pat on the back, high fives, and holding hands.

hug   person

CHAPTER 3:
LANGUAGE & COMMUNICATION
BENCHMARKS

Sign language enhances both language and communication skills for all young children. According to Dr. Marilyn Daniels, the foremost authority on the brain and academic benefits of sign language, sign offers parents and caregivers a unique opportunity to communicate in an effortless way with babies and young children. Further, her research shows hearing children who used sign in their pre-kindergarten and kindergarten classes scored better on vocabulary tests and attained higher reading levels than their non-signing peers.

Babies can learn sign language because they understand symbolic communication before they can form words with their mouths. Infants can understand their parents long before their parents understand them. This occurs because they have the motor control to make the signs. However, the vocal apparatus to form speech develops more slowly than the manual dexterity to form signs.

The added benefits of signing derive in part from its unique status as both a visual and kinetic language. There are individual memory stores for each language a person knows, even at the initial stages of acquiring the second or third language. You intake sign with your eyes, using the right side of the brain. Then like any other language, sign is processed and stored in the brain's left hemisphere. This operation creates more synapses in the brain, adding to its growth

and development. This process also helps to establish two memory stores in the left hemisphere for language, one for English (or the native language) and one for ASL. So children who use both develop a built-in redundancy of memory, storing the same word in two formats in two places. This enhances recall and speeds the learning of concepts.

Language & Communication Learning & Development Standards - Birth to Four

Sign Language Use as it Correlates to the Standards:
Word=Signs/Actions/Gestures

Language & Communication Benchmarks - Birth-8 Months

Communication & Speaking
1. Uses a variety of sounds and movements to communicate

2. Shows enjoyment of the sounds and rhythms of language

Emergent Writing

1. Develops eye-hand coordination and more intentional hand control
2. Watches activities of others and imitates sounds, facial expressions and actions

Listening & Understanding

1. Responds to frequently heard sounds and words

Language & Communication Benchmarks - 8-18 Months
Communication & Speaking

1. Uses consistent sounds, and gestures, and some words to communicate

Emergent Reading
1. Builds and uses vocabulary with language, pictures, and books

Emergent Writing

1. Develops eye-hand coordination and more intentional hand control
2. Watches activities of others and imitates sounds, facial expressions and actions

Listening & Understanding

1. Shows increased understanding and gestures and words

Language & Communication Benchmarks - 18-24 Months – Toddlers
Communication & Speaking

1. Attends to and tries to take part in conversations
2. Uses a number of words and uses words together

Emergent Reading

1. Learns that pictures represent objects, events and ideas (stories)
2. Shows motivation to read

Emergent Writing

1. Uses beginning representation through play that imitates familiar routines

Listening & Understanding

1. Gains meaning through listening

Language & Communication Benchmarks - 2-Year Olds
Communication & Speaking

1. Participates in conversations
2. Speaks clearly enough to be understood by most listeners.
3. Uses more complicated imitative play as symbolic thought processes and mental concepts or pictures are developed

Emergent Reading

1. Shows growing interest in print and books
2. Shows motivation to read.

Emergent Writing

1. Uses scribbles, marks, and drawings to convey messages

Listening & Understanding

1. Gains meaning through listening

Language & Communication Benchmarks - 2-Year Olds
Communication & Speaking

1. Shows improving expressive communication skills
2. Shows increased vocabulary and uses language for many purposes

Emergent Reading

1. Demonstrates beginning phonological awareness
2. Demonstrates comprehension and responds to stories
3. Shows an appreciation and enjoyment of reading
4. Shows awareness of letters and symbols

Emergent Writing

1. Begins to use writing, pictures, and play to express ideas
2. Shows beginning writing skills by making letter-like shapes and scribbles to write

Listening & Understanding

1. Listens to and understands spoken language
2. Shows understanding by following simple directions

Three Channels of Communication

1. Body Language (Crossed arms, Eye contact, Smiles, Etc.)

2. Tone & Modulation (Emotion, Volume, Tone, Etc.)

3. Words (Spoken, Written, Listened, Read)

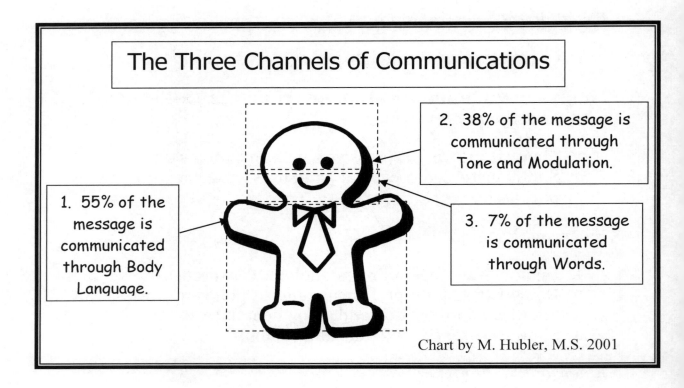

The Three Channels of Communications

1. 55% of the message is communicated through Body Language.

2. 38% of the message is communicated through Tone and Modulation.

3. 7% of the message is communicated through Words.

Chart by M. Hubler, M.S. 2001

VERBAL COMMUNICATION:

   Effectively combining the three channels improves communication.

   Inconsistent use of the Three Channels of Communication can impede the transmission of your message.

LISTENING SKILLS AND COMMUNICATION HINTS

Empathic Listening

☝ Is to identify with and/or understand the person you are listening to emotionally and intellectually.

Benefits

☝ Empathic listening enables us to better understand others' frame of reference.

☝ Empathic listening fosters meaningful communication and creates close relationships.

☝ Empathic listening invites the speaker to tell their story and release their feelings.

When Using Empathic Listening You hear/See...

☝ ...what the other person says

☝ ...understand what others really mean.

☝ ...the ideas the speaker is conveying.

☝ ...what people think is important.

When using Empathic Listening You...

☝ ...are aware of non-verbal communication.

☝ ...use appropriate tone & modulation.

☝ ...select the correct words to communicate.

☝ ...are able to listen to, and comprehend, the speaker's frame of reference.

COMMUNICATION HINTS

🖐 Listen Attentively

🖐 Establish Rapport

🖐 Communicate Openly and Honestly

🖐 Listen Empathically

🖐 Be Specific About What You Want or Need

🖐 Give and Receive Positive Feedback

🖐 Use "I" Phrases

SIGNING WITH CHILDREN

When Do I Start Signing with My Child?

🖐 You can begin signing with your child at birth. Start with some key basic signs to meet children's wants and needs. For example, you should begin with signs such as: eat, more, drink, please, and milk. Of course, if your child or class is beyond that age then start when you receive this book. The answer should always be now is the best time to start. The sooner the better, but we never wish to discourage a potential new signing educator or parent, rather we want them to start right away to attain the most benefits possible for their children.

🖐 Begin with one or two signs then work your way up to a few more. Don't be discouraged if your child(ren) seemingly doesn't notice your signs. Be consistent! One day the children will simply produce their first signs.

🖐 As you see the children begin to use their first few signs regularly, begin introducing additional signs. Be sure to observe children's cues, and practice introducing signs slowly, clearly, and in context.

Children learn best when everyone who is caring for them uses the same signs the same way. "Mixed-message" signs can frustrate children.   Repetition and consistency are the key factors for children's learning.

When are Children Ready to Sign?

When children attain enough motor coordination they will begin to respond. Generally, 7 months is the average for children to begin signing back their first signs.

When children have been exposed to a sign on a daily basis and have had time to practice processing its meaning.

When children demonstrate an active desire to communicate – pointing, vocalizing with tone & modulation (babbling or jabbering sounds; conversational or inquisitive), grunting while pointing at object/person, and other attempts at physical or visual cues to get attention or to enlist assistance. Indeed, it is perfectly natural for children to gesture with their hands to get their needs met, we are simply adding meaning to that gesturing.

When is the Best Time to Teach a Sign?

"Quiet Alert" State – Infants in this state provide a lot of pleasure and positive feedback for caregivers. It is the best time to provide infants with stimulation and learning opportunities. In this state children will display the following characteristics:
- Minimal body activity
- Brightening and widening of eyes
- Faces have bright, shining, sparkling looks
- Regular breathing pattern
- Curious about their environment, focusing attention on any stimuli that are present

In context –Children are perpetually ***"in the moment."*** For learning to occur, it must be connected or associated to a current event. For example, just prior to offering more milk (bottle or nursing), use the signs for "more milk." Repeated, consistent use of a sign in context will allow children to begin making the connection on their own. Then they will try to imitate the sign themselves. Eventually, they'll respond to your signs for "more milk" by gesturing or signing "yes" or "no."

Eye "Gaze" Contact – Use these opportunities to focus children's attention on some person/object/event and you at the same time, wait a moment, introduce (or repeat) a sign, say the word while signing it at the sight line between you and the child. This provides the "context" to "associate" learning and "make meaning."

Gazes

Expressive Gaze: Children look at you to communicate wants, needs, thoughts, or feelings.

Chance Mutual Gaze: Children's eyes and your eyes meet without intent or particular reason.

Pointed Gaze: Some event or sound causes a child and you to first look in the same direction for its source (person/thing/event) – Next, you both turn and look at each other.

INCORPORATING AMERICAN SIGN LANGUAGE INTO YOUR DAILY ROUTINE

- Learn the signs for some of the traditional songs that you sing with your children.

- Use common signs with infants, particularly during feeding times to help them learn to communicate while they are pre-verbal. Words such as eat, milk, more, drink, hurt, cold, and hot are easy to sign and particularly useful for the pre-verbal child.

- Sign the alphabet.

- Sign the numbers throughout the day (circle time, head counts, lunch counts).

- Sign the names of foods and manners at mealtimes.

- Teach children to sign the colors and encourage them to use both the sign and the word when naming colors.

- Teach the children to fingerspell their names.

- Teach the children signs for common actions: eat, play, sing, jump, walk and dance.

- Reduce aggression in your classroom by teaching children signs for emotions and manner signs, and signs for common words that they can use if they get frustrated or angry such as: please, thank you, welcome, angry, no, stop, mine, and help. This will reduce the noise level in the classroom as well.

- Teach the children how to sign the names of animals that you discuss in your classroom.

- Use the signs for words commonly used during daily interactions with children such as: mommy, daddy, work, and home.

- Teach the children to sign "potty" when they need to use the restroom. This will help to reduce the number of interruptions you experience during the day.

- Teachers can use non-verbal cues such a "no" or "stop" across the classroom without having to raise their voices or interrupt a conversation.

CHAPTER 4:
COMMUNICATION MILESTONES
& DEVELOPMENTALLY
APPROPRORIATE SIGNS

LEARNING SIGNS AS I GROW!

Birth to 6 Months

DEVELOPMENTAL MILESTONES

- Crying is primary form of communication
- Responds to sound
- Vocalizes sounds – gurgling and cooing
- Follows objects
- Smiles and laughs
- Recognizes faces and scents
- Coos when you talk to them
- Prefers human faces to all other patterns and colors
- Can distinguish between bold colors
- Amuses themselves by playing with hands and feet
- Turns toward sounds and voices
- Imitates sounds, blows bubbles
- Squeals
- Recognizes own name

SIGNS

milk	up	hear
more	finish/all gone	mother
eat/food	water	father
diaper change	bottle	baby

Birth–6 MONTHS SIGNS (ENGLISH/SPANISH)

baby – criatura, bebé

Place the dominant hand in the crook of the reference hand and make a gentle rocking motion from side to side.

As if cradling a baby in your arms.

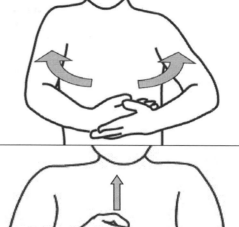

bottle - botella

The reference open hand is held palm up. The dominant "C" hand moves from on the reference hand up. As if holding a bottle in your hands.

[also: cup, glass]

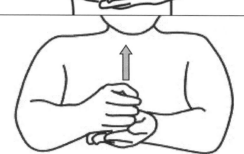

change diaper – cambiar el pañal

With both modified "X" hands, place the dominant "X" so the palm faces forward, with the reference "X" facing it. Twist the hands around until they have reversed positions. Start with both "U" handshapes pointing up, palm facing out, move both "U" handouts down to the hip palm facing in.
[also: adjust, adapt]

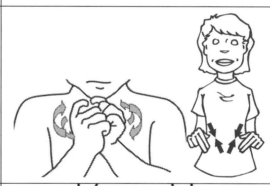

eat - comer

With the thumb and fingertips together, palm facing down, repeatedly move the fingertips towards the lip with short movements.

As if putting food in ones mouth.

father - padre

Place the thumb of the dominant "5" hand on the forehead.

Birth–6 MONTHS SIGNS (CONTINUED)

finish – fin, acabar

Hold the "5" hands in front of you, palms facing you, quickly twist hands to palms down.

[also: finished, completed, done, ended, over]

hear, oír, escuchar

Point the index finger towards the ear.

As if showing the ear to listen.

[also: ear]

milk - leche

Begin with the "C" hand in front of the body, tighten the hand to an "S" shape, repeatedly.

[As if milking a cow.]

more - más

Bring the tips of both "flat O" hands together twice.

mother - madre

Place the thumb of the "5" hand on the chin.

Birth -6 MONTHS SIGNS (CONTINUED)

# up – hacia arriba Point up with the index finger of the dominant hand.	
# water - agua Touch the mouth with the index finger of the "W" hand a few times.	

ACTIVITIES

- Read books, sign songs daily, include lullabies
- Introduce new vocabulary/signs in a meaningful context
- Speak directly to child – Wait – Give them time to respond
- Support "conversation" – Turn taking social/language skills
- Visual stimulation
- Body language games (This Little Piggy, Head and Shoulders)
- Environmental sounds (bring carrier while you do dishes, laundry, explain noises)
- Change child's position to give different perspective (sling, carrier, high chair, and floor)
- Give baby lots of opportunities for "tummy-time"
- Play peek-a-boo
- Encourage vocal play (vowel sounds "ooo" "aaah", consonant-vowel ba… da… Building to consonant-vowel-consonant: bababa … gagaga)
- Have "gooooo gooooo parties" or blow raspberries at each other…
- Introduce animals and their signs via puppets and stuffed animals

7 to 12 Months
DEVELOPMENTAL MILESTONES

- Imitates speech sounds – babbles

- Says "dada" and "mama"

- Combines syllables into word-like sounds

- Waves "bye-bye"

- Plays pat-a-cake

- Imitates others' activities

- Produces word-like sounds

- Indicates wants with gestures

- Responds to name and understands "no"

- Begins to say additional word or two – other than "mama" and "dada"

- Understands and responds to simple instructions

- Sits without support

SIGNS

banana	please	book
bath	thank you	hurt
drink	shoes	head
help	ear ache	socks
hot	no touch	jump

7-12 MONTHS SIGNS (ENGLISH/SPANISH)

banana - plátano
Move the closed fingertips of the dominant hand, down the extended reference index finger.

As if peeling your index finger.

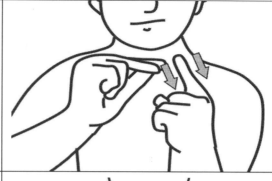

bath -baño
For wash rub the "A" hands together palm to palm.

For bath rub the "A" hands on the chest near the shoulder.

[also: scrub, wash]

book - libro
Starting with both palms touching in front of the chest, fingers pointing forward, move the hands apart, keeping the little fingers together.

As if opening a book.

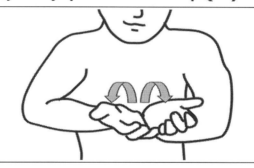

drink – bebida, tomar, beber
Use the "C" hand in front of the mouth and thumb touching bottom lip; then keeping the thumb in place, move fingers upward toward the nose.

As if taking a drink with the hands.

earache – dolor de oídos
Jab both index fingers toward each other several times in front of ear.

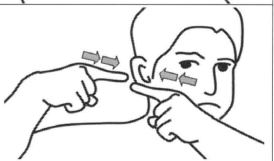

7-12 MONTHS SIGNS (CONTINUED)

head - cabeza

Place the fingertips of the dominant bent hand against the same-sided temple and then move the dominant hand downward in an arc to the jaw.

help - ayuda

Place the dominant open hand under the reference "A" hand, thumb up, lift both hands together.

[also: aid, assist]

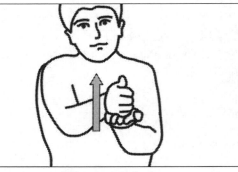

hot - caliente

Place the dominant "C" hand at the mouth, palm facing in; give the wrist a quick twist, so the palm faces out.

[also: heat]

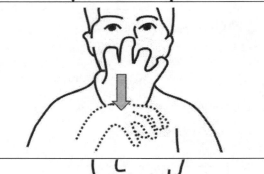

hurt - dolor

The index fingers are jabbed toward each other several times.

[also: pain, ache]

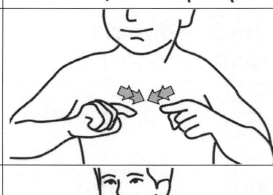

jump – saltar, brincar

Place the dominant "V" handshape in a standing position on the reference palm; lift the "V", bending the knuckles and return to a standing position.

7-12 MONTHS SIGNS (CONTINUED)

please – por favor
Rub the chest with the open hand in a circular motion (palm facing yourself)

As if rubbing your heart.
[also: pleasure, enjoy, like]

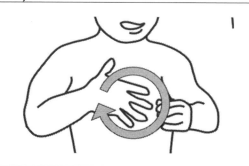

shoes -zapatos
Strike the sides of the "S" hands together several times.

socks – calcetín
Place the index fingers side-by-side and rub them back and forth several times, tilting downwards.

As if two knitting needles are making socks.

[also: stockings, hose]

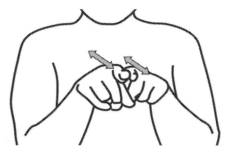

thank you - gracias
Touch lips with the fingertips of flat hand, then move the hand forward until the palm is facing up and towards the indicated person. Smile and nod head while doing this sign.

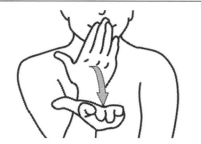

touch – toque, tocar
Touch the back of the reference hand with the dominant middle finger, other fingers extended.

no touch - Shake your head no while making the touch sign.

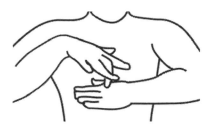

ACTIVITIES

- Books!! Books!!! – Build story time routines, especially at bedtime! Children who are read to nightly have been shown to make 25% more than their non-nightly reading counterparts upon reaching adulthood

- Baby's own picture book – Make it with Grandma or Grandpa!

- Give back baby's words using adult language

- Naming walks around house/outside

- Bath time play

- Animal sounds – songs like Animals on the Farm and Old MacDonald

- Puppets are great fun for language play/games – Make your own from paper bags or socks – use non-toxic markers. Recycle the paper – wash the socks for more play!

- Body parts – Play exercise games touching baby's foot to hands – alternate right hand with left foot – Make reference to top of body vs. bottom of body; left side and right side; use position words such as "up" and "down"

- Mirror games

- All gone games

- Grab bag games

13 to 18 Months

DEVELOPMENTAL MILESTONES

- Uses two words skillfully – e.g., "hi", "bye"
- Imitates others
- Vocabulary increases, uses words more often
- Turns the pages of a book
- Enjoys pretend games
- Will "read" board books on his own
- Scribbles well
- Enjoys gazing at their reflection
- Plays "peek-a-boo"
- Points to one body part when asked
- Adopts "no" as their favorite word
- Responds to directions – "Sit down"
- Speaks more clearly
- Strings words together in phrases

SIGNS

moon	stop	airplane
hug	where	want
mine	yes	apple
no	fish	dog
toilet	cookie	bed

13-18 MONTHS SIGNS (ENGLISH/SPANISH)

airplane – aeroplano, avión

Use the "Y" hand, with index finger extended and palm facing down. Make forward upward sweeping motion.

As if flying an airplane across the sky.

apple - manzana

With the knuckle of the bent index finger on the dominant cheek, twist downward.

bed – cama, acostarse

Place the slightly curved dominant hand on the same-sided cheek and tilt the head to the side.

As if laying down your head on the hand.

cookie - galleta

Touch the fingers of the dominant clawed "5" hand on the upturned reference palm and then twist the dominant hand and touch the reference palm again.

As if cutting cookies with a cookie cutter.

dog - perro

Snap the middle finger against the thumb. Can also add slapping the upper leg.

As if calling a dog.

13-18 MONTHS SIGNS (CONTINUED)

fish - pez
Begin with the dominant open hand palm facing the reference side and the reference extended index finger on the heel of the dominant hand. Swing the dominant hand back and forth with a double movement.

Like a fish swimming.

hug- abrazo, abrazar
The hands hold the upper arms as if hugging yourself.

mine - mío
Place the dominant open hand on the chest.

moon - luna
Tap the thumb of the modified "C" hand over the dominant eye, palm facing forward, with a double movement.

The symbol represents the crescent moon.

no - no
Bring the index, middle finger, and thumb together in one motion.

13-18 MONTHS SIGNS (CONTINUED)

stop – parar, alto, detener, poner fin Bring the little finger side of the dominant open hand abruptly down on the upturned reference palm. As if chopping on something.	
toilet – tocador, cuarto de baño, inodoro Shake the dominant "T" hand from side to side in front of the body, palm facing forward.	
want – necesitar, querer Place both "curved 5" hands in front of you, palms up, and draw them towards you. As if gesturing to bring something to you.	
where - dónde Hold up the dominant index finger and shake the hand back and forth quickly from reference to dominant.	
yes - sí Shake the "S" hand up and down in front of you.	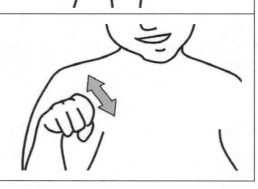

ACTIVITIES

- Ball Play – Rolling back and forth; throwing/bouncing (sponge and soft balls)

- Music Games – Finger play (Itsy Bitsy Spider)

- Books!!! – Reading to Child

- Animal "Talk" – Trips to zoo/farm – "Let's move/walk/sound like an elephant…monkey…kangaroo, etc."

- Pretend Play – Imitate Daily Living Activities

- Pull/push/ride toys

- Conversation games (jargon is child imitating adult intonation pattern)

- Blocks – Stacking toys; nesting and sorting toys

- Flash cards with animals and common objects

- Grab bag

- Coloring – Supervised

- Water color – Use plain water with paintbrush on sidewalk. Or, if you need to be inside – paint the Sunday comics (they'll feel like their painting and the comics are in color!)

- Shaving cream on tabletop or cookie sheet – great sensory activity – Careful to keep hands out of mouth and eyes!

- Finger paint with pudding – Use vanilla flavor and add food coloring to make a few choices.

19 to 24 Months

DEVELOPMENTAL MILESTONES

- Recognizes when something is stated incorrectly – e.g. someone calls a cat a dog
- Learns words at a rate of 10 or more a day
- Searches for hidden objects
- Follows two-step requests – "Get your toy and bring it here"
- Can name a simple picture in a book
- Can use 50 single words
- Half of speech is understandable
- Produces short sentences
- Capable of identifying several body parts
- Produces two or three word sentences
- Sings simple tunes
- Begins talking about self

SIGNS

happy	butterfly	wait
rain	friend	car
cat	bird	fish
cold	telephone	hard
soft	sad	rough
angry		

19-24 MONTHS SIGNS (ENGLISH/SPANISH)

angry – colérico , enojado, enfadado

Place the clawed "5" hands against the waist and draw up against the sides of the body.

As if anger is boiling up out of person.

[also: wrath]

bird - pájaro

With the "G" hand at the mouth, palm forward, repeatedly open and close the index finger.

As if displaying a birds beak.

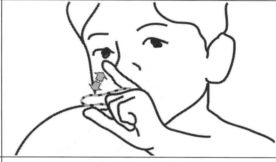

butterfly - mariposa

With the hands crossed at the wrist, palms toward the chest, and the thumbs of the open hands hooked together, flex and straighten several times.

As if demonstrating how a butterfly's wings flutter.

car – carro, coche, auto

Place the "S" hands in front of you, palms facing each other, and alternate clockwise then counter- clockwise as if driving a car.

As if steering a car.

[also: automobile, drive]

cat – gato(a)

The "F" hand touches the corner of the upper lip, brushing out and away from the face a couple of times.

As if you are stroking a cat's whiskers.

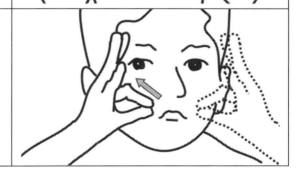

19-24 MONTHS SIGNS (CONTINUED)

# cold - frio Shake both "S" hands, palms facing each other. "Brr!"	
# fish - pez Begin with the dominant open hand palm facing the reference side and the reference extended index finger on the heel of the dominant hand. Swing the dominant hand back and forth with a double movement. Like a fish swimming.	
# friend – amigo(a) Interlock dominant "X" hand index finger down over upturned reference "X" hand index finger. As if holding hands with someone.	
# happy – alegre, feliz, contento The open hands pat the chest several times with a slight upward motion. As if heart is pounding with joy. [also: glad, rejoice, joy]	
# hard – duro, difícil With both hands in the "bent V" handshape, tap the dominant hand on the reference hand. Palms facing in the opposite direction.	

19-24 MONTHS SIGNS (CONTINUED)

rain - lluvia

Let both curved "5" hands, palms facing down, drop down several times in short, quick motions.

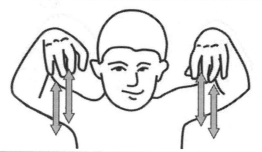

rough - tosco

Move the fingertips of the dominant curved 5 hand, palm facing down, from the heel to the fingertips of the upturned reference open hand.

sad - triste

Hold both open hands in front of the face, fingers slightly apart and pointing up; then drop both hands a short distance and bend the head slightly.

[also: dejected, sorrowful, downcast]

soft – blando, ablandar, suave

Beginning with both "flat O" handshape in front of the shoulders, bring the hands down with a double movement while rubbing the fingers against the thumbs each time.

As if the fingers are feeling soft.

telephone - teléfono

Place the thumb of the "Y" hand on the ear and the little finger at the mouth.

As if talking on the phone.

[also: call]

19-24 MONTHS SIGNS (CONTINUED)

wait – espera, esperar

Beginning with both curved "5" hands in front of the body, reference palm up in front of the dominant palm up, wiggle the fingers.

As if asking for something.

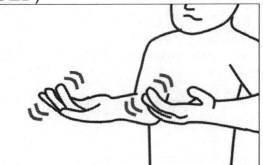

ACTIVITIES

- Happy/sad emotion face games

- Hide objects behind your back – Which hand? – "shell games"

- Books!!! Books!!! Use puppets to retell stories – extend and make up your own stories!

- Dress up and dramatic play games

- Cars – Trains – Provide lots of containers for them to use and blocks to make roads.

- Hide-and-seek – Introduce counting – very simple rules.

- Texture boxes – Cut scraps from old clothing with interesting and different materials.

- Sensory Play – Sand/water/dough/pudding, etc.

- Water Play – Use dolls in bathtub to name body parts – bath, brush teeth and hair – build social and self-help skills.

- Painting/Coloring activities – support play – support language and conversation – describe what your child is doing and what you are doing – Play with your child. Get on the floor with them!

25 to 30 Months

DEVELOPMENTAL MILESTONES

- Names several body parts
- Speaks clearly most to all of the time
- Understands emotional expressions
- Answers "wh" questions
- Uses up to 200 words
- Asks simple questions
- Comprehends up to 500 words
- Listens to a 5-10 minute story

SIGNS

cow	good	monkey	stop
down	grandmother	snake	throw
fish	hide	snow	toilet
frog	horse	sorry	work

25-30 MONTHS SIGNS (ENGLISH/SPANISH)

cow - vaca

With the thumbs of the "Y" hands at the temples, bend the wrists forward a few times. Shows a cow's horns.

As if showing a bull's horns.

down - abajo

Point down with the index finger.

frog - rana

Begin with "S" hand under the chin, flick the index and middle fingers outward.

As if to indicate the filling of air into the frog's throat.

good – bueno(a), bien

Starting with fingertips of the open hand on the lips, move the hand down to touch the open palm.

As if something tasted good and you want more.

grandmother - abuela

Sign "mother". Place the thumb of the "5" hand on the chin, then bounce forward once.

Indicates one generation away from mother.

25-30 MONTHS SIGNS (CONTINUED)

hide – esconder, esconderse, ocultar

Move the thumb of the dominant "A" hand under the reference curved hand, palm facing down. Gesture putting something under the other hand as if to hide it.

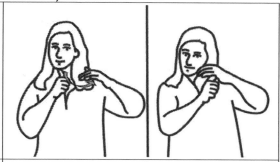

horse - caballo

With the "U" hand beside the temple, bend and unbend the index and middle fingers.

Indicates a horse's ears.

monkey - mono

Scratch the ribs on both sides of the body with the curved "5" hands.

As if scratching characteristics of monkeys.

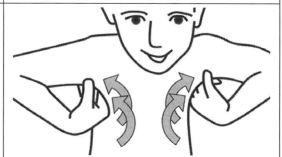

snake – culebra, serpiente

Sharply move the "bent V" handshape in a spiral movement.

Indicates a snake preparing to strike with its fangs.

snow - nieve

Let both "5" hands, palm down, drop down while gently wiggling the fingers.

As if snowflakes pointing downward.

25-30 MONTHS SIGNS (CONTINUED)

sorry – lo siento, lo lamento Rub the palm side of the dominant "S" hand in a large circle on the chest with a repeated movement. Indicates rubbing the heart in sorrow.	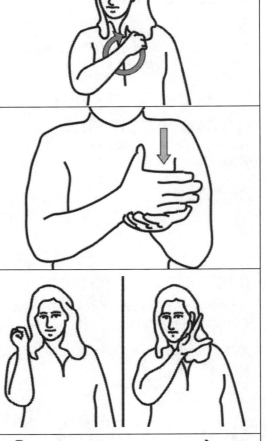
stop – alto, parar, detener, poner fin Bring the little finger side of the dominant open hand abruptly down on the upturned reference palm. As if chopping on something.	
throw – tirar, lanzar, aventar Beginning with the dominant "S" hand in front of the dominant shoulder, move the hand forward and downward while opening into a 5 hand. As if throwing something.	
walk – paseo, andar, caminar Open hands, palms down, are moved in a forward-downward motion alternately As if walking with the hands.	

ACTIVITIES

- Sorting, matching, and counting games -- Use large craft buttons, blocks, etc.)

- In/on, over/under games – Hide and seek with objects.

- Books!!! Books!!!! Make your own books about family trips – daily routines – grocery shopping – going to the park, etc.

- Eye-hand coordination activities – Support fine and gross motor skills. Bean bag toss at a target; drop clothespins in a plastic bottle. Help your child to get them out – it's harder than it looks!

- "Once upon a Story…." – Together you and your child make up stories "on-the-spot" by taking turns adding 1-2 sentences each – building upon each other's pieces. Tape record the stories as you both get better and replay them later. Send them to relatives for presents!

- Make a tape w/ different sounds around the house

- "Simon Says" games – These are very fun when you're trying to get some chores done around the house – or cleaning out old toys.

- Make your own video with your child telling story, signing song, and then let them watch it. Also, makes a great gift for family and friends.

31 to 36 Months

DEVELOPMENTAL MILESTONES

- Names six or more body parts
- Names one color
- Carries on conversations of two to three sentences
- Describes how two objects are used
- Uses four to five words in a sentence
- Uses prepositions – on, in, over
- Follows a two or three part command
- Uses up to 500 words
- Comprehends up to 900 words
- Listens to 10 minute story
- Understands simple comparisons – big/little
- Repeats common rhymes

SIGNS

bear	coat	paper	square
bee	circle	pink	turtle
black	colors	purple	warm
blue	dance	rabbit	white
boy	flower	red	yellow
brother	girl	sister	
brown	orange	sit	

31-36 MONTHS SIGNS (ENGLISH/SPANISH)

bear – oso, osa Scratch the upper chest near the shoulders repeatedly with both "5" hands crossed in front of chest at the wrists. As if giving a bear hug.	
bee - abeja Press the "F" hand against the dominant cheek. Then brush the index-finger side of the dominant "B" hand against the cheek. Indicating the biting action of an insect then a natural gesture of brushing it away.	
black - negro Beginning with the center of the forehead, draw the index finger across the eyebrow.	
blue - azul Shake the dominant "B" hand in front of the chest.	
boy – niño, chico, muchacho Beginning with the index-finger side of the dominant "C" hand near the dominant side of the forehead, close the fingers to the thumb with a repeated movement. As if grasping the visor of a baseball cap.	

31-36 MONTHS SIGNS (CONTINUED)

brother - hermano

Sign "BOY" and "SAME".
First move with the index-finger side of the dominant "C" hand near the dominant side of the forehead, close the fingers to the thumb with a repeated movement. Then place both index fingers side by side, pointing to the front.

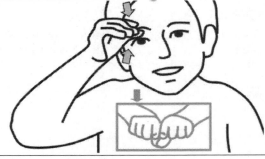

brown – marrón, color café

Move the index-finger side of the "B" hand down the dominant cheek.

circle - círculo

Beginning with the "1" hand in front of the top of the chest, palm facing out, move the hand in a circular motion all the way back to point at which you began.

As if drawing a circle.

coat - abrigo

Bring the thumbs of both A hands from near each shoulder, palms facing in, downward and toward each other, ending near the waist.

Indicates a coat's lapels.

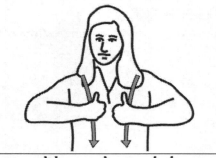

colors – colores, color

Place the "5" hand in front of the mouth and wiggle the fingers as the hand moves away slightly.

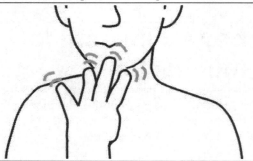

31-36 MONTHS SIGNS (CONTINUED)

# dance - baile Place the "V" in the standing position on the reference palm and swing the "V" back and forth. As if dancing with the fingers.	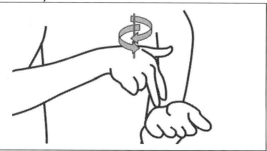
# flower - flor First place the tips of the "flat O" hand first under one nostril, then under the other. As if smelling a flower.	
# girl – niña, chica, muchacha Move the thumb of the dominant A hand, downward on the dominant cheek to the dominant side of the chin.	
# orange – naranja Squeeze the "S" hand once or twice at the chin. Sign for the color the fruit. [Same sign for color or fruit] # orange – anaranjado Squeeze the "S" hand once or twice at the chin. Sign for the color orange.	
# paper – papel Sweep the heel of the dominant "5" hand, palm down, back against the heel of the upturned reference "5" hand with an upward motion, in a double movement.	

31-36 MONTHS SIGNS (CONTINUED)

pink – rosa Brush the middle finger of the dominant "P" hand, palm facing in, downward across the lips with a short repeated movement.	
purple – púrpura, morado Gently shake the fingers of the "P" handshape.	
rabbit – conejo With the "U" hands crossed above the wrists, palms facing in and thumbs extended, bend the fingers of both hands forward and back towards the chest with a double movement. Indicates the rabbit's ears.	
red - rojo Move the inside tip of the dominant index finger down across the lips. Also, made with an "R" handshape.	
sit - sentarse Place the fingers of the "H" hand on top of the reference "H" hand, palms facing down, as if sitting on a bench. As if two legs are dangling from a bench.	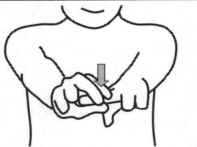

31-36 MONTHS SIGNS (CONTINUED)

# sister - hermana Sign "GIRL", then "SAME". First move the thumb of the dominant "A" hand, palm facing reference, downward on the dominant cheek to the dominant side of the chin. Then place both index fingers side by side, pointing to the front.	
# square – cuadro, cuadrado With the dominant index finger, in front of the dominant shoulder, bring the dominant hand down, then to your reference, then up in front of your reference shoulder, then back across your body to where you began.	
# turtle - tortuga Cup the reference palm over the dominant "A" hand and wiggle the dominant thumb with a repeated movement. As if the turtle's head is coming out of its shell.	
# yellow - amarillo Gently shake the "Y" handshape at chest level.	
# warm – calído Beginning with the fingers of the dominant "E" hand near the mouth, palm facing in, move the hand forward in a small arc while opening the fingers into a C hand. Indicates the warm air coming from the mouth.	

31-36 MONTHS SIGNS (CONTINUED)

white - blanco
Place fingertips of the "5" hand on the chest and move the hand forward into the flattened "O" hand.

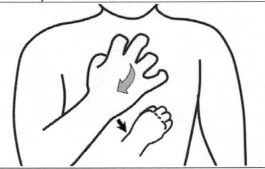

ACTIVITIES

- Tricycle – "big wheel" riding and peddle toy play

- Toilet Mastery – stories, introduce "potty language" and steps for using the toilet, e.g., pulling down pants, sitting, wiping, washing hands, etc.

- Activities that build on location words: in, on, under, top.

- Use comparison words: big/little, rough/smooth.

- Bean Bag Toss

- Felt Board Sequencing Activities

- Rhyming Stories/Poems – Mother Goose stories

- Color matching and sorting activities

- Connective Blocks – Building patterns with blocks

- Puzzles – Floor and table top – easy interlocking

- Shape sorters

- Coloring – Cutting and pasting – Arts 'n Crafts

- Simply cooking activities – great for language development and social/self help skills building.

37 to 42 Months

DEVELOPMENTAL MILESTONES

- Engages in longer dialogue
- Requests permission – "May I?"
- Corrects others when they misspeak
- Clarifies own conversation when misunderstood
- Uses up to 800 words
- Answers simple "how" questions
- Uses compound sentences with "and"
- Comprehends 1,200 words
- Emerging understanding of location – "in front of", "behind"
- Recognizes simple comparisons – hard/soft, rough/smooth
- Recognizes the names of simple shapes – circle, square

SIGNS

book	little	popcorn	Teacher
doctor	nurse	potato	Teacher's Aide
Firefighter	over	scared	tickle
game	out	scissors	tired
glue	play	spider	under
ice cream	police	spoon	worm
lion			

37-42 MONTHS SIGNS (ENGLISH/SPANISH)

book - libro

Starting with both palms touching in front of the chest, fingers pointing forward, move the hands apart, keeping the little fingers together.

As if opening a book.

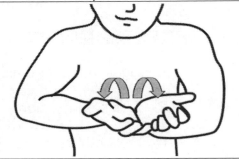

doctor – doctor(ora), médico

Tap the reference wrist, palm facing up, with the dominant "D" hand with a double movement.

As if taking your pulse.

firefighter - bombero

Bring the back of the dominant "B" hand, fingers pointing up and palm facing forward, against the center of the forehead.

Represents the raised front of the firefighter's helmet.

game – juego, jugar

Bring the "A" hands towards each other, palms toward the body, in a slightly upward motion.

As if two people are facing each other in competition.

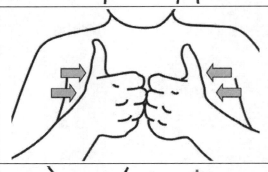

glue – cola de pegar, pega

Move the fingertips of the dominant "G" hand, palm and fingers facing down in a circular movement over the upturned reference open hand.

You can fingerspell G-L-U-E.

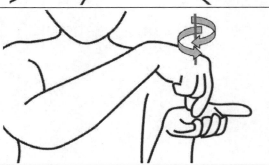

37-42 MONTHS SIGNS (CONTINUED)

ice cream - helado Bring the index-finger side of the dominant "S" hand, back in an arc towards the mouth with a double movement. Indicates eating an ice cream cone.	
lion - león Beginning with the fingers of the dominant curved "5" hand pointing down over the forehead, move the hand back over the top of the head. Indicates the lions mane.	
little – pequeño, poco Bring your hands close together as if to clap, stopping about 1" from touching. Indicates size.	
nurse - enfermera Tap the extended fingers of the dominant N hand with a double movement on the wrist of the reference open hand held in front of the body, palm facing up. As if checking your pulse.	
out – fuera The dominant "open 5" hand, facing the body and pointing down, becomes a "flat O" hand as it moves up through the reference "C" which then becomes an "O".	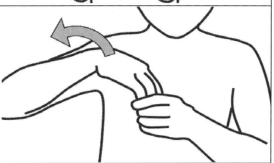

37-42 MONTHS SIGNS (CONTINUED)

over – encima de, sobre, arriba de With the fingertips of both bent hands touching in front of the chest, move the dominant hand up in a short arc.	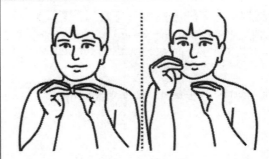
play – juego, jugar Place the "Y" hands in front of you and shake them in and out from the wrist a few times. Indicates play as in recreation.	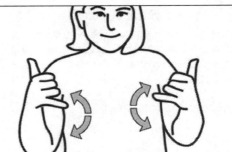
Police Officer - policía Tap the thumb side of the dominant modified "C" hand, against the reference side of the chest with a double movement. Indicates the badge.	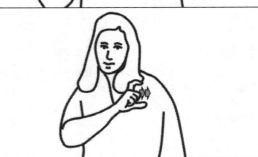
popcorn – palomitas de maíz Beginning with both "S" hands in front of each side of the body, alternatively move each hand upward while flicking out each index finger with a repeated movement. Indicates the location of the police badge.	
potato – papas, patata Tap the fingertips of the dominant bent "V" hand, with a double movement on the back of the reference open hand. Indicates putting fork tines into a baked potato to see if it is done.	

37-42 MONTHS SIGNS (CONTINUED)

scared – tener miedo, alarmar

Begin with both "A" hands in front of each side of the chest, spread the fingers open with a quick movement changing into "5" hands, palms facing in and fingers pointing toward each other.

[also: scared, frightened, terrify]

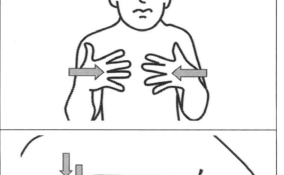

scissors - tijera

With the "H" hand turned, palm facing self, open and close fingers repeatedly.

As if your hand was a pair of scissors.

spoon - cuchara

Wipe the backs of the fingers of the dominant "U" hand, palm facing up and thumb extended, across the upturned palm of the reference opened hand from the fingers to the heel.

Indicates a spoon scooping up food.

spider - araña

With the hands crossed at the wrists, palms down, wriggle the fingers of both "claw" hands. Show the spider's legs crawling.

Indicates the leg movement of a spider.

Teacher, teach – maetra(o), enseñar

Move both "flattened O" hands, forward with a small double movement in front of each side of the head. Then with both open hands facing each other in front of the chest move them down to in front of the waist.

Sign "teach + "agent"

The hands seem to take information from the head and direct it to another person.

37-42 MONTHS SIGNS (CONTINUED)

Teacher's Aide – maestro(a) asistente

First move both flattened "O" hands, palms facing each other, forward with a small double movement in front of each side of the head. [The hands seem to take information from the head and direct it from another person.]
Then use the thumb of the dominant "A" hand under the little-finger side of the reference "A" hand to push the reference hand upward in front of the chest. [Hands show a boost being given.]

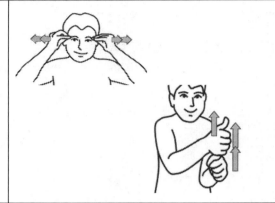

tickle - cosquilla

Wiggle the fingers of both curved "5" hands in front of each shoulder.

Indicates the act of tickling a person.

tired – cansado(a)

Fingertips of the bent hands are placed at each side of the body just inside the shoulders and then dropped slightly.

Indicates the shoulders falling forward when tired.

[also: weary, exhausted]

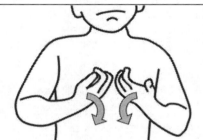

under – abajo de, debajo de

Move the dominant "A" hand under the open reference hand, palm facing down.

Indicates being under something else.

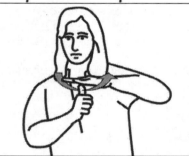

worm – gusano, lombriz

Make the dominant bent index finger, palm facing forward, inch forward against the palm of the reference hand, palm facing dominant side, as it wiggles.

Indicates a worm inching along.

67 Teaching: Sign Language for the Early Childhood Environment

ACTIVITIES

- Cooking activities (cut off cookies, say utensils 1st, then, next)

- Board Games – Cards – Dominos. All with simple rules.

- Books!!!! – Especially those with repeating and rhyming phrases.

- Counting games (drop in the bucket, barrel full of monkeys)

- Play who/what games

- Cut and pasting activities using shapes – Sponge painting -- make a collage from magazine cutouts.

- Dramatic Play – Different occupations/jobs – Lot's of language opportunities.

- Make a huge tent with blanket and chairs and talk about what is in the woods. Pretend you're all on a far away planet and tell what it's like in this strange, new place.

- Simon Says (2 actions), Mother May I? Red Light Green Light

- Rhyming games

- Texture bag

- Grab bag – Add story-building game as your child guesses what the object is or what it's used for.

- Treasure Hunt – Scavenger Hunt

Copyright © 2014 Time to Sign, Inc.

43 to 48 Months

DEVELOPMENTAL MILESTONES

- Speech is more fluid and understandable
- Uses up to 1,000 – 1,500 words
- Comprehends up to 1,500 – 2,000 words
- Begins to understand the difference between fiction/non-fiction
- Uses more details in conversation
- Emerging ability to accurately discuss topics/events, e.g. "out of context"
- Effectively uses vocabulary to express personal thoughts – discusses emotions and feelings
- Narrative and retelling skills – able to tell and sequence story or situation events, emerging understanding of characters and character development
- Emerging use of conjunctions – "because"
- Emerging use of reflexive pronouns – "myself"

SIGNS

clouds	head	pig	sheep
cake	home	reading	sun
delicious	nap-time	run	thunder
elephant	pie	share	

43-48 MONTHS SIGNS (ENGLISH/SPANISH)

cloud(s) - nube

Begin with both "C" hands near the reference side of the head, palms facing each other, bring the hands away from each other in outward arcs while turning the palms in. Repeat near the dominant side of the head.

Shape and location of clouds.

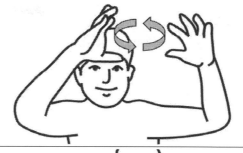

cake - pastel

Beginning with the fingertips of the curved dominant "5" hand on the palm of the reference open hand, raise the dominant hand upward.

Indicates a cake rising.

delicious - delicioso

Touch the bent middle finger of the dominant 5 hand to the lips, palm facing in, and then twist the dominant hand quickly forward.

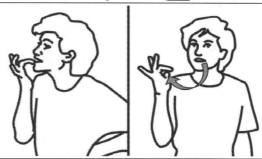

elephant - elefante

Starting with the bent open hand at the nose, fingers pointing forward and palm down, swoop the hand downward, ending forward movement at the chest level.

Indicates an elephant's trunk.

head - cabeza

Place the fingertips of the dominant bent hand against the same-sided temple and then move the dominant hand downward in an arc to the jaw.

43-48 MONTHS SIGNS (CONTINUED)

home – hogar, casa
Place the tips of the "flat O" hand against the mouth and then the cheek (or, place the flat hand on the cheek.)

nap-time – siesta, sueñecito
Place the slightly curved dominant hand on the dominant cheek and tilt the head to the dominant side.

As if laying down your head on the hand.

[also: bed]

pie – pastel, torta
Slide the fingertips of the dominant open hand, palm facing reference, from the fingers to the heel of the upturned reference hand, fingers pointing forward, and then perpendicularly across the reference palm.

Indicates cutting a pie into slices.

[Can also be used with a "C" hand for cake]

pig – cerdo, puerco
With the back of the dominant open hand, under the chin, palm facing down, bend the dominant fingers down, and then up again with a double movement.

read - leer
Move the fingertips of the dominant "V" hand, palm facing down, from the thumb to the little finger of the reference open hand.

Indicates the movement of the eyes down a page to read it.

43-48 MONTHS SIGNS (CONTINUED)

### run - correr Hook the index of the dominant "L" under the thumb of the reference "L" and move the hands forward in a quick short motion.	
### share – compartir, participar Open dominant hand is placed in the crook of the open reference hand and moves back and forth as if cutting a portion of something to share. As if cutting a portion.	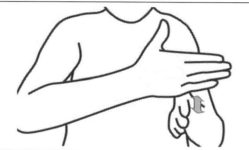
### sheep - oveja Slide the back of the fingers of the dominant "V" hand, palm facing up from the wrist up the inside of the forearm of the reference bent arm with a short repeated movement.	
### sun - sol **The "C" hand is held at the dominant temple and extended forward and upward.**	
### thunder – trueno, tronar Touch the extended dominant index finger to the dominant ear. Then shake both "S" hands from side to side with a repeated movement in front of each shoulder.	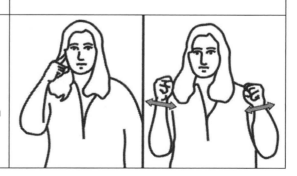

ACTIVITIES

- Daily schedule – Sequence events – Routine activities

- "What if….." stories. Support descriptive language use and problem solving skills – "If my ice cream fell off the cone, I would feel _____. But, then I could _____" Include opportunities for "fact" or "fable" stories. "If I were King, I would …… Then, I would….."

- Turn taking stories – Build on from one day to the next. Supports comprehension and retention/retelling skills.

- Dressing self dolls…buttons, Velcro, undergarments, ties

- Simon Says (3 actions)

- Nature hunt – explore ponds, back yard, trails, etc.

- Petting farms – Age-appropriate plays, concerts, fairs, etc

- Circle games

- Drama activities for children

49 to 60 Months

DEVELOPMENTAL MILESTONES

- Connected speech and language understandable
- Uses "what do…does…did" questions
- Uses 1,500 to 2,000 words
- Answers simple "when" questions
- Retells long story with increasing accuracy
- Knows and can state full name – first, middle, last
- Reflexive pronouns emerging more consistently
- Comparatives vs. superlatives emerging – "-er," "-est"
- Uses 5 to 8 word sentences
- Developing understanding of prepositions – between, above, below, bottom
- Repeats the days of the week
- Emerging ability to name months – knows birthday (day and month)

SIGNS

baseball	grandfather	Monday	Friday
catch	hug	Tuesday	Saturday
dirty	say	Wednesday	Sunday
dream	soccer	Thursday	
go	welcome		
grandmother			

49-60 MONTHS SIGNS (ENGLISH/SPANISH)

baseball - béisbol

With the little finger of the dominant "S" hand on the index finger of the reference "S" hand, palms facing in opposite directions, move the hands from near the dominant shoulder downward in an arc across the front of the body.

Natural gesture of swinging a baseball bat.

catch, coger, agarrar

Move the dominant curved hand into the reference curved "5" hand in front of the chest.

Indicates receiving a ball into a glove.

dirty – sucio, cochino

With the back of the dominant open hand, under the chin, palm facing down, wiggle the fingers.

dream - sueño

Move the extended dominant index finger from the dominant side of the forehead, outward and upward to the dominant hand while bending the finger up and down.

Indicates an image coming from the mind.

go – irse, marchar, andar

Begin with both hands raised in front of the chest with the index finger pointing up, then move both hands simultaneously to the reference side in a downward arc movement.

49-60 MONTHS SIGNS (CONTINUED)

grandfather - abuelo

Sign "father". Place the thumb of the dominant "5" hand on the forehead. then bounce forward from forehead once.

Origin: One generation away from father.

grandmother - abuela

Sign "mother". Place the thumb of the "5" hand on the chin, then bounce forward once.

Origin: One generation away from mother.

hug - abrazo

The hands hold the upper arms as if hugging yourself.

say – dicho, decir, aserto

The index finger, held in front of the mouth, moves forward towards the person being addressed.

[also: speak, say, tell, speech]

soccer - fútbol

Flick the index finger of the dominant hand on the open palm of the reference hand.

49-60 MONTHS SIGNS (CONTINUED)

welcome – bienvenido(a) Bring the upturned dominant curved hand from in front of the dominant side of the body in toward the center of the waist. **You are welcome – de nada**	
Monday - Lunes [Initialized sign] Move the dominant "M" hand, palm facing in, in a double circle in front of the dominant shoulder.	
Tuesday - Martes [Initialized sign] Move the dominant "T" hand, palm facing in, in a circle in front of the dominant shoulder.	
Wednesday - Miércoles [Initialize sign] Move the dominant "W" hand, palm facing out and fingers pointing up, in a circle in front of the dominant shoulder.	
Thursday - Jueves [Abbreviation "T" + "H"] Beginning with the dominant "T" hand in front of the dominant shoulder, palm facing forward in a small circle, quickly switch to the "H" hand and continue the circle.	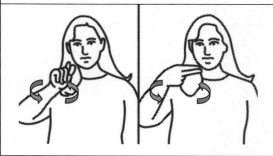

49-60 MONTHS SIGNS (CONTINUED)

Friday - Viernes

[Initialized sign]
Move the dominant "F" hand, palm facing in, in a repeated circle in front of the dominant shoulder.

Saturday - Sábado

[Initialized sign]
Move the dominant "S" hand, palm facing out, in a small circle in front of the dominant shoulder.

Sunday - Domingo

[The movement of the hands shows reverence and awe]
Beginning with both open hands in front of each shoulder, palms facing forward and fingers pointing up, move the hands forward in small inward circles.

Time to Sign inc.

ACTIVITIES

- Big/bigger/biggest comparison games

- Dominoes, board games, card games – with increasing number of rules and complexity

- Puzzles and building blocks – More complex – smaller pieces – larger number of pieces, etc. 3-D puzzles are great – Your help playing and putting things together is an essential part of supporting your child's schema building – problem solving and higher level thinking, etc.

- What's missing? – What did I take away? Games with cards, or silly/ordinary objects.

- What's wrong with this picture? Supports connection between cognitive and language building skills.

- Advanced concentration/memory games

- Make a calendar – or Daily Routine Chart

- Pretend play with money – store scenarios that build basic money concepts and mathematical reasoning skills. "If you have 10 cents, you could have….." (10 pennies, or 2 nickels, or 5 pennies and 1 nickel, or 1 dime), etc. Make change using quarters only or quarters and dollar bills. To add to the fun make your own pretend money – Put your own picture on the coins!

CHAPTER 5:
ACTIVITIES & SIGNS TO ENHANCE THE
CLASSROOM & BEHAVIORAL MANAGEMENT

Let's Work Together

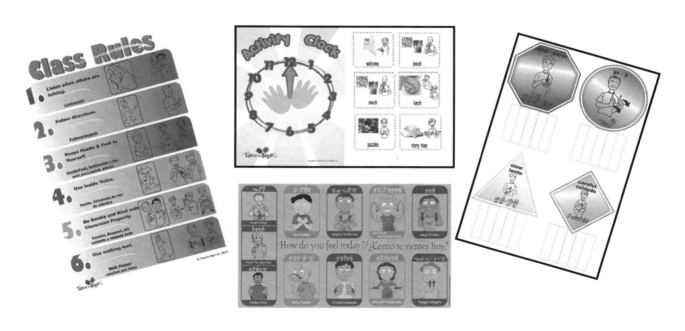

Alphabet

- Fingerspell Names -- Teach your child how to fingerspell his/her name.
- Hokey Pokey to ABC's -- Use your child's first letter of his/her name as follows:
    You put your (child's name first letter) in
    You put your (the letter) out
    You put your (child's name first letter) in
    And you shake it all about
    You do the hokey pokey and (say your child's name) turn yourselves around
    That's what it's all about
- Alphabet Animals -- Learn ABC to Animals (A-Z) – Sit in a circle, use the ABC to Animals chart and teach your children the animals that correspond with the letter. Then sign and sing A for Alligator, B for Bear, C for Cat, etc.
- Favorite Animal Initial -- Sit in a circle and have your children tell you the name of their favorite animal. Help them form the finger alphabet letter of the animal or sign the favorite animal's name. Everyone learns how to sign everyone's favorites as you go around the circle.
- BINGO -- Sing and sign the song *Bingo*:
    There was a farmer that had a dog and Bingo was his name O
    B-I-N-G-O (say and fingerspell)
    B-I-N-G-O (say and fingerspell)
    B-I-N-G-O (say and fingerspell)
    And Bingo was his name O (then take a letter off each round)

Classroom

- Labeling –Label your classroom with the name and sign for the object (chair, table, cubby, desk, door, etc.). This promotes literacy.
- Counting-- Discuss the different items in the classroom (counting how many chairs, tables, windows).
- Where in the Room is ...? (Game) – Select an item, use the sign for the item, and call on a quiet hand to guess the item.
- Clean-up Fun -- Use the sign for an item and assign a helper to put that item away (crayons, glue, paper, toys, etc.).

Classroom Phrases

- Transitions—Sign phrases for daily transitions: circle time, clean up time, outside/inside, nap time, play time, work time, snack time, story time, eat time, and our favorite Time to Sign!
- Directional Phrases -- Use signs for classroom management such as: use manners, use words, walk please, inside voices, time to go, share, and wash your hands.

Colors

- I Spy Colors –Teach children the sign s for the basic colors. Play I Spy using the learned signs. "I spy with my one good eye _____ (sign)".
- Traffic Light -- Use signs for red, green and yellow to teach children about classroom management color usage. Label areas in the color red for stop, color green for go, and color yellow for slow.
- Bean Bags -- Use Color Bean Bags and toss and sign the different colors.
- Art Coloring -- Teach children the colors and then use painting or arts and craft activities for children to ask for different color crayons to use. "May I have the _____ (sign color) crayon".
- Sorting -- Use signs in classroom color sorting activities (sort the blues or yellows).
- What Color Am I Wearing? Ask your children to sign the colors in their clothing.

Emotions

- Happy and Sad Activity -- Sit in a circle. Give your child two paper plates. One with a sad face and one with a happy face. Have them choose between happy and sad as you read emotion sentences. Here are some examples to choose from: *I dropped my ice cream on the ground*", " *I got a new toy.*", "*I got to each my favorite food.*", "*I got hurt.*", "*I am going to the playground*", "*I went to the zoo*", or "*I got a big lollipop*".
- My Emotions -- Sit in a circle. Teach your children signs for the following emotions: angry, happy, excited, love, sad, and tired. You can show pictures of each emotion. Have the children respond to the appropriate sign to each of the following "What if?" stories: *"There is a lightning storm outside, how do you feel?", "The new boy took my favorite toy out of my hand.", "My friend is coming to play with me.", or "Mommy gives me hugs."*
- Emotions Art Activity -- Give children a piece of paper and have them draw a card with a face on it showing emotions for that person.
- Role Playing -- Guide your child in how to display emotions in situations that occur. For example, when my brother takes my toy, sign and say "mommy help me" or "sharing".

Greetings and Manners

- Role Model -- Being an example is the best way to teach good manners.
- Greetings -- Use signs to greet the children and use the signs for manners.
- Manners -- Routinely say yes please or no thank you.

Numbers

- 🖐 Simple Counting Games – Sign the numbers 1-20:
  - ○ Use dice to introduce the numbers (roll the dice and then sign the number on the dice)
  - ○ Count the number of small blocks and then build something with the blocks. Then count how many blocks are in a stack or in a row.
  - ○ Count the pieces of a small puzzle. Then put the puzzle together.
- 🖐 <u>Three Little Monkeys</u> -- Finger play and sign the numbers to the *3 Little Monkeys Swinging in a Tree* song:

  Three little monkeys swinging in a tree
  Teasing Mr. Alligator can't catch me
  Along came the alligator quite as can be
  And snatched that monkey out the tree
  (then 2, then 1, then no little monkeys swinging in a tree)
- 🖐 <u>Play with Counting</u> -- Count items at home, at school, on walks, anywhere you go.
- 🖐 <u>Number Cards</u> -- Use number cards for the visual effect. Sign the numbers as you count.
- 🖐 <u>Beans in a Jar</u> -- Place a small number of items (beans, pencils, paper clips) in a jar, and ask your children to guess how many items are in the jar. Empty the jar and count each beans verbally along with the signs.
- 🖐 <u>Counting Cheese Fish Cracker</u> -- Give each child 5 cheese fish crackers. To make each fish disappear, instruct your children to eat one cracker at a time. Recite the following rhyme:

  Five little fish in the deep blue sea, swimming along happily
  Along comes a whale, as quiet as can be
  And snatches a fishy right out of the sea (Repeat for 4, 3, 2, 1)
- 🖐 <u>Five Little Snowman Finger Play </u>-- Teach your child this poem about snowmen, signing the key words or numbers from 1-5:

  Five little snowman standing in a row, each had a hat and a big red bow
  Out came the sun and it shone all day and one little snowman melted away. (Continue with 4, 3, 2, and 1 until they all melted away)

Questions

- 🖐 Use asking questions to ensure that they understand a story, game, or activity. Including what was the story about, who is the person in the story, where did the story take place, etc.
- 🖐 Questions stimulate cognitive thought. Where did it go?, What time is it?, Who is here today?, When are we eating, How are you feeling?, etc.

Classroom Signs

bed – cama, acostarse, dormir Place the slightly curved dominant "5" handshape on the same-sided cheek and tilt the head to the side. [As if laying down your head on the hand]	
chair - silla Place the fingers of the "H" handshape on top of the reference "H" handshape, palms facing down, as if sitting on a bench. [As if two legs are dangling from a bench]	
crayon – crayon, lapiz de color Place the "5" handshape in front of the mouth and wiggle the fingers as the hand moves away slightly.	
cubbies – cubículo Start with both hands facing one another, palms in and shoulder length apart, move both hands simultaneously 90 degrees to form both sides of a box.	
desk – escritorio, mésa Start with the dominant hand raised slightly above the reference arm, move the dominant arm down onto the reference arm. Then have both hands touching in front of the chest, palms facing down, move the hands apart, then down, to imitate the form of the desk.	

Classroom Signs

door – puerta Start with both hands facing up and touching in front of the chest, move the dominant hand out while turning sideways.	
games – juego Bring the "A" handshapes towards each other, palms facing the body, in a double movement. [As if two people facing each other in competition]	
glue – cola para pegar, pega Move the fingertips of the dominant "G" hand-shape, palm and fingers facing down in a circular movement over the upturned reference open hand. [You can also fingerspell G-L-U-E]	
paper – papel Sweep the heel of the dominant "5" handshape, palm down, back against the heel of the up-turned reference "5" handshape with an up-ward motion.	
puppets – marioneta Start with both hands in front of the body with palms forward and the middle-finger pointed down, dominant hand just slightly above the reference hand, move hand up and down in alternating pattern. [As if pulling up and down on the puppets strings]	

Classroom Signs

puzzles – rompecabezas Start with the extended fingertips of both "H" handshapes touching in front of the chest, dominant palm facing forward and reference palm facing in, twist the hands in opposite directions to reverse positions with a double movement.	
scissors - tijera With the "H" handshape turned, palm facing in towards the body, open and close fingers repeatedly as if your hand was a pair of scissors. [Wrist motion, finger motion]	
school - escuela Tap the fingers of the dominant open hand, palm facing down, with a double movement of the upturned palm of the reference open hand.	
shelf – estante Start with the index-finger sides of both "B" handshapes touching in front of the chest, palms facing down and fingers pointing forward, bring the hands apart to in front of each side of the chest.	
table – mésa Start with the dominant hand raised slightly above the reference arm, move the dominant arm down onto the reference arm.	

Classroom Signs

teach – enseñar Move both "flattened O" hands, forward with a small double movement in front of each side of the head. [Teacher ends with the "er" (person) modifier] [The hands seem to take information from the head and direct it to another person]	
toilet – tocador, cuarto de baño Shake the "T" for bathroom or the "R" hand-shape for restroom.	
toys – juguete Start with the "T" handshapes facing one another, shake repeatedly back and forth.	
water table – mésa de agua Touch the mouth with the index finger of the "W" handshape a few times. Then with the dominant hand raised slightly above the reference arm, move the dominant arm down onto the reference arm.	
window – ventana Start with the dominant "5" handshape just above the reference "5" handshape, fingers pointing in opposite directions, bring the little finger side of the dominant open hand down sharply with a double movement on the index-finger side of the reference open hand.	

Common Classroom Phrases

sit in a circle - sentarse en circulo

sit in a circle

clean up time - tiempo de limpiar, vamos a limpiar

clean up   time

come here please/now - venga aquí por favor

come here   please   now

Common Classroom Phrases

don't throw/push - no tire, no empujes

don't   throw   push

time to go inside - tiempo de ir adentro, tiempo de entrar, vamos a dentro

time   go   inside

Time to go outside - tiempo ir afuera , vamos afuera

time   go   outside

Common Classroom Phrases

good work - buen trabajo

good   work

terrific - tremendo

terrific/wonderful

I am proud of you - estoy orgulloso (a) de ti

I   proud   you

let's line up - vamos a ponernos en fila, ponerse en fila

let's   line up

Common Classroom Phrases

Common Classroom Phrases

careful please - tengan cuidado por favor

careful   please

please keep your hands to yourself - por favor, mantenga las manos quietas

please   keep   hands   yourself

please sit still - sientese quieto por favor

please   sit   still

Common Classroom Phrases

Common Classroom Phrases

say you are sorry	I'm Sorry
- digale que lo siento	- perdóname, disculpame
- lo siento digale perdón, pidale perdón	

say   sorry   I'm   sorry

share please - compartír por favor

share   please

snack time - tiempo de comer un bocado, hora de la merienda

snack   time

Common Classroom Phrases

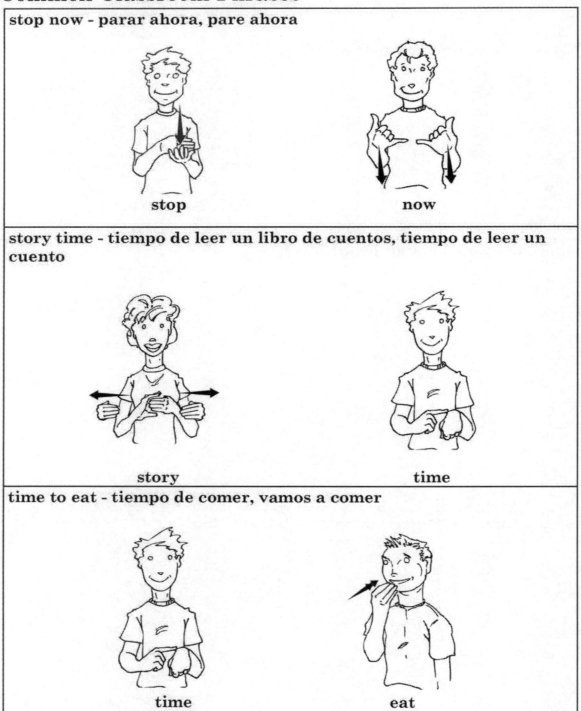

stop now - parar ahora, pare ahora

stop   now

story time - tiempo de leer un libro de cuentos, tiempo de leer un cuento

story   time

time to eat - tiempo de comer, vamos a comer

time   eat

Common Classroom Phrases

Common Classroom Phrases

Common Classroom Phrases

wash your hands - lavarse sus manos

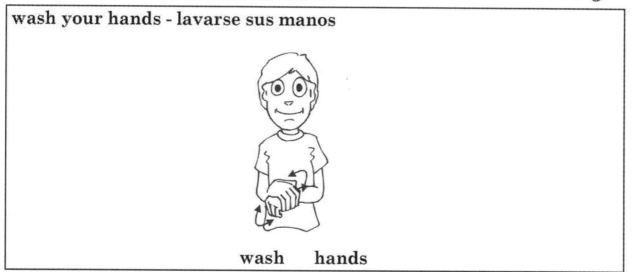

wash   hands

CHAPTER 6:
SIGNING WITH YOUNG CHILDREN
WITH SPECIAL NEEDS

LEARNING SIGN LANGUAGE TO AUGMENT COMMUNICATION AND LEARNING WITH OUR SPECIAL NEEDS CHILDREN

Who uses American Sign Language?

Sign language is a system of communication that is typically used with hearing and hearing-impaired (deaf and hard of hearing) individuals of all ages as their primary form of communication. All children have a need to learn how to communicate. Some children with special needs are hindered in their ability to communicate verbally. Sign language is a wonderful alternative communication tool that has been shown to enhance communication for children who have special needs such as:

- Apraxia
- Attention Deficit Disorder (ADD) and Attention Deficit Hyperactivity Disorder (ADHD)
- Autism
- Cerebral Palsy
- Down Syndrome
- Deafness/Hearing Impairment
- Language Learning Disability (LLD) and
- Various Other Learning Delays or Impairment

Autism

What is Autism?

Autism is a developmental disorder which can form in the first three years of life. It affects brain development, impacting social and communication skills. This can make it difficult for children to understand others and to express themselves. As many as 1 in 88 children have been identified with an autism spectrum disorder (ASD) according to estimates from CDC's Autism and Developmental Disabilities Monitoring (ADDM) Network.

With few exceptions, researchers have been able to clearly and repeatedly demonstrate that sign language improved communication performance for children with Autism. Further, some children with severe Autism were able to enhance functional communication by being taught basic signs.

Why does American Sign Language help children with Autism?

Children with Autism are visual learners, as their primary language is pictorial, rather than verbal. Sign language is a pictorial representation that a child can more easily understand. Also, once learned, sign language can help a child to stay focused so they may understand what is being communicated. Additionally, children with autism tend to be much more literal. They may be confused by sarcasm, puns, hints, or slang words; which are not a part of sign language.

Down Syndrome

What is Down Syndrome?

Down syndrome is a common genetic variation of chromosome 21 that results in physical, intellectual, and language development delays. The CDC estimates that Down syndrome affects approximately 1 out of 700 babies born each year in the United States. (http://www.cdc.gov/ncbddd/birthdefects/DownSyndrome.html)

Why does American Sign Language help children with Down Syndrome?

Each child is unique. Speech is not the only way to communicate. Hearing children who have speech and language delays often use sign language as a communication system. Sign language is effective for visual learners because signing is a pictorial representation that a child can easily understand.

Using sign language as a helpful communication system, actually helps enhance spoken language communication. In other words we should use sign language and speech together. Why? Researchers have determined that using sign language stimulates the parts of the brain associated with speech and language development. Think of sign language as a communication bridge to speech and language acquisition that positively impacts social and emotional (behavioral), and academic learning.

Children can become frustrated when their need is not met. Down syndrome children may need more time to process information or limits set on the amount of information given at one time. They may need support to help make seamless transitions between activities to stay on task. Some special needs children also have challenges processing relevant information to determine the proper social response. Sign language can help children stay focused on what is being communicated.

Studies have shown that when all students, including children with special needs, are taught in the general classrooms, they do better socially, emotionally and academically.

ADHD

What is ADHD?

Children with Attention Deficit Hyperactivity Disorder (ADHD) may exhibit symptoms such as difficulty paying attention, hyperactivity, and impulsiveness. The National Institute of Mental Health estimates that 3% - 5% of all children have ADHD, while some experts estimate it's as high as 10%.

Why Does Sign Language Help Children with ADHD?

Researchers have been able to demonstrate that sign language is a great tool to use in teaching language to children with ADHD because they tend to be visual learners. Sign language is a pictorial representation that a child can easily understand. Children who consistently move around need movement in their day. Signing is a way to communicate in a more active yet controlled manner.

Signing develops the ability to focus because one must look at the signer to know what is being communicated. Since sign language requires children to focus on making the signs, this allows for a better control of impulsive behavior. Children using sign language to communicate are calmer and spend less time interrupting others. Studies show that children using sign language are learning more and are more productive in the classroom with fewer interruptions.

Children who often experience difficulty understanding what parents and teachers want also tend to have difficulty expressing their own needs and desires. Many negative behaviors such as aggression, bullying, tantrums, self-injury, anxiety, and depression can be the result of, or intensified by, a child's difficulty or inability to communicate their basic needs and wants. After all, who doesn't get frustrated if they are consistently not understood? Sign language can enhance communication, ease frustration and result in more positive expressions of behavior.

Things your special needs child wants you to know:

- I forget things – It is very important to establish clear guidelines and expectations. Be consistent. Doing the same thing at the same time helps me remember.

- I am easily distracted – Prepare a quiet environment, away from distractions, for doing tasks that require concentration.

- I am very smart – I need time to organize my thoughts before speaking. Write down your expectations and let me know exactly what you would like me to do.

- I ask a lot of questions – In order for me to process and comprehend what you are saying; I ask a lot of questions. I also ask questions to make a mental picture to remember what I need to do.

- I need to know how I am doing – Please tell me what I am doing right and reward good behavior. Give me positive input and role model actions that I can imitate.

- I need help to succeed – Help me when I am struggling because I don't often ask for help.

- I learn differently – To learn I need to ask questions. I need repetition, guidance, and routines.

Why use sign language with children who have special needs?

Children with special needs often experience difficulty understanding what parents and teachers want and also they have difficulty expressing their own needs. Many negative behaviors such as aggression, bullying, tantrums, self-injury, anxiety, and depression can be the result of, or intensified by, a child's difficulty or inability to communicate their basic needs and wants. After all who doesn't get frustrated if they are consistently not understood? When sign language is used to enhance communication, it can also ease frustration and result in more positive expressions of behavior.

Sign language can be an augmentative communication system, which actually helps to enhance spoken communication. In other words we should use sign language and speech together. Why? Researchers have determined that using sign language stimulates the parts of the brain associated with speech and language development. Think of sign language as a communication bridge to speech and language acquisition that positively impacts behavior and academic learning.

Speech and Language Benefits of Sign Language for Special Needs Children

1.   Sign language accelerates the acquisition of speech by stimulating areas of the brain that are associated with speech and language.

2.   Babies develop the gross motor skills needed for signing long before they develop the fine motor skills associated with verbal speech.

3.   Signing provides language stimulation and conceptual information that enhances vocabulary development in children.

4.   Many children with special needs experience difficulty with expressive language and verbal communication. Sign language gives these children access to communication while strengthening the ability to produce expressive speech. A connection is made between the object and its label.

Emotional Benefits of Sign Language for Special Needs Children

1.   By expanding vocabulary, social opportunities, and opportunities for success in learning sign language enhances self esteem.

2.   Children who face communication barriers benefit greatly when they are provided with various accesses to language and learning. Enhancing communication promotes opportunities for socialization and social awareness.

3.   Children develop better communication skills through sign language; which in turn makes them more independent, enables play through enhanced social capabilities, and subsequently makes them happier. They have fun with their friends.

Social Benefits of Sign Language for Special Needs Children

1.   Sign language is a pictorial representation that enhances understanding and functional communication. This in turn leads to increased and more successful play opportunities with peers.

2.   Since sign language is a pictorial representation, parents can understand their child and respond more quickly to their needs. Meeting a young child's

needs immediately reduces their frustration and makes them happier; which in turn promotes friendly behavior and treatment of others around them.

3.   Sign language reduces frustration by providing a way to expressively communicate in situations where verbal communication may not be successful; thereby enhancing their peer, parent, and teacher interactions.

4.   Sign language breaks down communication barriers for children with various disabilities and needs. Removing these barriers facilitates play and socialization opportunities.

Academic Benefits of Sign Language for Special Needs Children

1.   Children begin to develop language from the time that they are born. The brain begins to make connections through both auditory and visual input.

2.   Children with special needs may have barriers that affect verbal communication skills. Sign language helps to overcome these barriers leading to enhanced communication, and social and emotional development. All of which better prepares your child to learn.

3.   Using both sign language and speech together can speed the learning process, as it adds redundancy, which facilitates quicker and better recall of words and concepts.

4.   Approximately 80% of signs are iconic or pictorial representations of what the sign represents. They are often easier to learn than the spoken word.

5.   Sign language enhances the development of pre and early literacy skills. It also helps young children with their mastery of ABC's and numbers.

6.   Sign language is a two-sided brain activity whereas hearing is not. This actually causes more synapses to fire up, in essence building the brain. Sign language has been shown to boost IQ's by as much as 12 points per child.

7.   Sign language essentially jump-starts the areas of the brain that are linked to speech and language development.

8.   Language is a primary building block for learning and academic development. Sign language stimulates intellectual development and helps children to retain information longer because it supplements speech input.

9.   Using many modes of input strengthens connections in the brain and therefore benefits academic development.

Should I Sign With My Special Needs Child?

An Early Interventionist or Speech-Language Pathologist is a great resource to consult with to determine if using sign language is appropriate for your child. Children with special needs often need to learn from more than one communication method (visual, auditory, and kinesthetic).

How Do I Start Using Sign Language with Children Who Have Special Needs?

Begin by teaching just a few simple words. Choose words that are meaningful and practical. It is so gratifying and significant to see recognition and understanding in a child who is a new signer. Some basic signs to start with are: eat, drink, more, hurt, and tired. Teach the signs for a favorite toy, food, or activities. Teach the signs for emotions to enable you to understand how your child is feeling. The use of the positive expression of emotions in sign enables your child to be rewarded by being understood; which in turn reinforces the positive behavior.

CHAPTER 7:
BASIC SIGNS FOR YOUNG & SPECIAL NEEDS CHILDREN

Basic Signs

clean, wipe/limpiar Move the palm of the dominant open hand from the heel to the fingers of the upturned palm of the reference open hand with a repeated movement. [Indicates wiping off something from your hands].	
change diaper/cambiar el pañal With both modified "X" handshapes, place the dominant "X" so the palm faces forward, with the reference "X" facing it. Twist the hands around until they have reversed positions. Diaper: Start with both "U" handshapes pointing up, palms facing out, move both "U" handshapes down to the hip palms facing in.	
cold/frío Shake both "S" handshapes, palms facing in each other, in front of the chest. [Indicating cold, "Brr"]	
dirty/sucio With the back of the dominant open hand, under the chin, palm facing down, wiggle the fingers.	
drink/beber [Wrist motion, face motion, palm motion, finger motion] Use the "C" handshape in front of the mouth, palm facing body and thumb touching bottom lip; then keeping the thumb in place, twist fingers upward toward the nose. As if taking a drink with the hands.	

Basic Signs

eat/comer With the thumb and fingertips together, palm facing down, repeatedly move the fingertips toward the lip with short movements. [As if putting food in ones mouth]	
finish/fin, acabar Begin with both "5" handshapes held in front of the chest, palm facing in and fingers pointing up, flip the hands over with sudden movement ending with both palms facing down and fingers pointing forward. [Also completed, done, ended, over]	
help/ayuda Place the open reference hand, palm facing upward, under the dominant "10" handshape, thumb up, lift both hands together. [Also: aid, assist]	
hot/caliente Place the dominant curved "5" handshape at the mouth, palm facing in; give the wrist a quick twist, so the palms face out. [Also heat]	
hungry/tienes hambre Start with the fingertips of the dominant "C" handshape, touching the center of the chest, palms facing in, move the hand downward a short distance. [Indicates an empty stomach]	

Basic Signs

I love you/te quiero, te amo With the dominant hand create a combination of the "Y" handshape, with the "L" handshape, palm facing forward in front of the dominant side of the body.	
in, inside/adentro Begin with the dominant open"5" handshape, facing the body and pointing down becomes a flat "O" handshape, as it moves in through the reference "C" handshape which then becomes an "O" handshape. **out, outside/afuera** Begin with the dominant open"5" handshape, facing the body and pointing down inserted in the reference "O" handshape, bring the dominant hand upward closing into a flattened "O" handshape.	
more/más [Two (2) - arm motion] Bring the tips of both "AND" hands together.	
no/no Bring the dominant index finger, middle finger and thumb together in one motion.	
open/abrir Begin both open "5" handshapes, in front of the body, palms facing out, move in a semi-circular motion to each side of the body. **close/cerrar** Begin both open "5" handshapes at the side of the body and move inward in a semi-circular motion and end in front of the body.	

Basic Signs

pain, hurt/dolor, doler Begin with both extended index fingers pointing toward each other in front of the chest, palms facing in, jab the fingers toward each other with a short repeated movement. [Also pain, ache] For questions: use your facial expression to ask a question, as are you hurt?, where does it hurt?	
sick, ill/enfermo Touch the bend middle finger of the dominant "5" handshape to the forehead, palm facing in, while touching the bent index finger of the reference "5" handshape to the chest.	
sit/sentarse Hook the fingers of the dominant curved "U" handshape, palm facing down, perpendicular to the fingers of the reference "U" handshape held in front of the chest, palm facing down and fingers pointing to dominant side. [Represents legs dangling from the edge of a seat]	
sleep, naptime/dormir, acostarse [Palm motion, arm motion) Place the slightly curved right hand on the right cheek and tilt the head to the right. [As if laying down your head on the hand]	**Routines help me feel safe.**
thirsty/tienes sed Move the extended dominant index finger, palm facing in and fingers pointing up, downward along the next, bending the finger down as it moves. [Indicates a dry throat]	

Basic Signs

touch, no touch/toque, no toque Touch the back of the reference hand with the dominant middle finger, other fingers extended, palms facing down. For no touch: shake your head no while making sign.	
toilet, potty/baño [Wrist motion, palm motion] Shake the dominant "T" handshape, palm facing forward held in front of the dominant shoulder. [Also: bathroom, toilet]	
wait/espera, esperar Beginning with both curved "5" handshapes in front of the body, reference palm in front of the dominant, palms facing up, wiggle all fingers.	
want/querer Place both "curved 5" hands in front of the chest, palms facing up, and draw towards you. [As if gesturing to bring something to you]	
yes/ sí Move the dominant "S" handshape, palm facing forward and held in front of the dominant shoulder, up and down by bending the wrist with a repeated movement. [As if nodding your fist]	

CHAPTER 8:
THEMES & LESSONS

PLAY & LEARNING

Young children learn through songs, games, stories, play, and interaction with others. Chapter 8: Themes & Lessons provides theme-based activities to incorporate into instructional lessons for young children. Each theme incorporates multiple learning modalities to reinforce learning of all areas of toddler and preschooler education, and social and emotional development. For specific outcomes and indicators regarding these activities in sign see the Time to Sign Early Childhood Education Curriculum available at www.timetosign.com .

<u>Age Appropriate Identification Key</u>

(I)=Infants
(T)=Toddler
(P)=Preschool
(S)=School Age

Activities, Songs, and Signs are available in the easy to use handouts in Chapter 10 Handouts.

Topic 1 - Play & Learn ABC's

(I)	Learn: ABC's (slowly sign ABC song) and basic signs (diaper, eat, drink, more, hurt)
(T/P/S)	Learn: Alphabet Fingerspelling (A-Z)
(I)	Activity: Show and Tell in a meaningful ways basic signs using objects
(T)	Activity: Hokey Pokey to ABC's
(P/S)	Activity: Fingerspell First Letter of Children's Names
(I/T/P/S)	Song: ABC's Song
(S)	Activity: Name Game
(T)	Activity: ABC Animals
(T/P)	Activity: Body Letters
(T/P)	Activity: Color letter of the week in the activity guide
(S)	Activity: Complete letter of the week activities in the activity guide
(T/P/S)	Art Activity: Finger paint using the alphabet signs learned today
(I/T/P)	Story: <u>1,2,3, to the Zoo</u>: A Counting Book by Eric Carle (zoo, animals, math)

*Time to Sign Props: Alphabet cards, ABC Wall poster and Infant Cards

Topic 2 - Play & Learn ABC's With Animals

(I)	Learn: Farm Animals and then teach basic signs (baby, I/me, no, yes, please)
(T/P/S)	Learn: Alphabet Fingerspelling (A-Z)
(I)	Song: Animals of the Farm
(T)	Song: ABC's song
(P/S)	Song: Bingo
(T/P/S)	Song/Chant: Who Came to Class Today? (use own tune-no music provided)
(P/S)	Play: Favorite Animal Initials
(T/P/S)	Learn: Animal signs – Animal Alphabet
(T/P)	Activity: Color the letter of the week page in the activity guide
(P/S)	Activity: Complete letter of the week activities in the activity guide

(T/P/S)   Art Activity: Use cotton balls and glue for children to create their favorite animals

(I/T/P/S)   Story: <u>Brown Bear</u> by Martin Jr. & Eric Carle (colors, animals)

*Time to Sign Props: Alphabet cards, ABC Wall poster, We See Stories (Bugs, Farm, Ocean, Pets, and Jungle) Infant Cards

Topic 3 - Play & Learn Manners

(I)   Learn: please, thank you, welcome and then sign basics (mom, dad, good)

(T)   Learn: Manners signs - Please, thank you, good, good morning, share

(P/S)   Learn: Manners signs - Excuse me, good, manners, may I?, please, thank you, you're welcome, good morning, good afternoon, good night, share

(I/T)   Song: Please & Thank You (to the tune of "are you sleeping")

(T/P/S)   Activity: Complete manners activity in the preschool activity guide

(P/S)   Song: Use your manners

(S)   Activity: Color the letter of the week pages in the activity guide

(P/S)   Activity: Complete letter of the week pages in the activity guide

(I/T/P/S)   Story: <u>The Children's Manners Book</u> by Alida Allison (manners)

*Time to Sign Props: Classroom Management cards

Topic 4 - Emotions

(I/T)   Learn: Emotion signs - Love, happy, sad, yes, no

(P/S)   Learn: Emotion signs - Afraid/scared, angry/mad, excited, feelings, happy, love

(T)   Activity: Cat Warm Up

(T/P)   Activity: Happy or Sad

(I/T/P/S)   Song: If You're Happy and You Know It

(T/P/S)   Activity: My Emotions

(S)   Song: Tell Me Why?

(T/P/S)   Song: The More We Sign Together

(S)   Activity: Color letter of the week page in the activity guide

(P/S)   Activity: Complete letter of the week and Emotions activities in the activity guide

(T/P/S)   Art Activity: Children will create a card to give to someone in the class showing their emotions for that person (ex: happy, silly, funny, sad...)

(I)   Story: <u>Baby Faces</u> by DK Publishing (emotions)

(T/P/S)   Story: <u>Arnie and the New Kid</u> by Nancy Carlson (feelings)

*Time to Sign Props: Emotions Poster, Seal Social Skills Poster, and Infant Cards

Topic 5 - Counting

(I)	Learn: Numbers from 1-10 and then teach basic signs diaper, eat, drink, more, hurt, sleep, baby, I/me, no, yes, please, thank you,
(I)	Song: 3 Little Monkeys
(T/P/S)	Learn: Counting – Numbers 1-10 (use Number cards with things that go)
(S)	Learn: Counting – Numbers 1-20 (use Number cards with things that go)
(T/P)	Song: 3-Little Monkeys, Ten Little Amigos or Ten Little Indians (use instrumental "10 Little Indians")
(S)	Song: The Ants Go Marching
(T/P)	Activity: Counting dice (role dice and count the dots. The number of dots you roll tells how many small blocks that child can play with.
(S)	Activity: complete "Adding Numbers in Sign Language" activity in activity guide
(P/S)	Song: Hands Can Count
(T/P/S)	Art Activity: Fruit Loops Fun! (Add fruit loops to a string to tie around the wrist. The children can count how many fruit loops they can fit on the string.)
(I)	Story: <u>Five Little Ducks</u> by Pamela Palarone (animals, counting, family)
(I/T/P/S)	Story: <u>Counting on the Woods</u> by George Ella Lyon (count, math, nature)

Time to Sign Props: Sign Language Number Cards, and Placemat Number Signs

Topic 6 – Counting 2

(I)	Learn: 1-10 and then teach basic signs (apple, banana, cookie, milk, help)
(T)	Learn: Numbers 1-10 again and try 11-15
(P/S)	Learn: Numbers 11-20
(T)	Activity: Letter of the week page in activity guide
(P)	Activity: Complete letter of the week and number activities in the activity guide
(S)	Activity: Complete letter of the week and "Find the Missing
(I/T/P)	Song: Three Little Monkeys
(T/P)	Song: Six Little Ducks
(T)	Activity: Waddle-a-way
(P/S)	Activity: Duck Relay
(T/P/S)	Activity: Counting Clothes
(I)	Story: <u>Five Little Monkeys Sitting in a Tree</u> by Eileen Christelow (math, animals)
(T/P/S)	Story: <u>Fish Eyes</u> by Lois Ehlert (math, animals)

Props: Sign Language Number Cards and Placemat Numbers Signs

Topic 7 - Farm Animals

(I)   Learn: Farm Animal signs - Pig, sheep, dog, cat, horse
(T/P/S)   Learn: Farm Animal signs - Cow, pig, sheep, horse, chicken, goat, duck, turkey
(T/P)   Activity: Cat Warm Up
(T/P)   Song: Animals on the Farm
(T/P)   Activity: Animal Hop
(T)   Activity: Color letter of the week page in activity guide
(P/S)   Activity: Complete letter of the week activities in the activity guide
(S)   Activity: Complete "Farm Animals and Pets Word Search" in the activity guide
(S)   Song: Old Mac Donald
(I/T/P/S) Story: <u>Farm Flu</u> by Teresa Bateman (farm animals)
   Time to Sign Prop: Sign Language ABC Animals Cards, ABC to Animals Poster, Farm Animals Story and Infant Cards

Topic 8 - Farm Signs 2

(I)   Learn: Farm signs - Cow, mouse, chicken, duck, turkey,
(T/P/S)   Learn: Farm signs - Apple, barn, corn, country, farm, farmer, eggs, feed, hay, milk, rice, tractor
(T/P)   Activity: Jumping Warm Up
(T/P/S)   Song: Old MacDonald
(S)   Activity: Circle Call Game (animals)
(T)   Activity: Color letter of the week page in activity guide
(P/S)   Activity: Complete letter of the week activities in the activity guide
(I/T/P/S) Story: <u>Cock-a-doodle-doo: A Farmyard Counting Book</u> by Steve Lavis (farm, animals, math)
(I/T/P/S) Story: <u>Old MacDonald</u> by David A. Carter (farm, animals)
   Time to Sign Prop: Sign Language ABC Animals Cards, ABC to Animals Poster, Farm Animals Story and Infant Cards

Topic 9 – Family

(I/T)   Learn: Family signs - Mother, father, baby, grandmother, grandfather, boy, girl
(P/S)   Learn: Family signs - Mother, father, baby, son, daughter, grandmother, grandfather, niece, nephew, uncle, aunt, cousin
(T/P)   Song: Happy Little Child
(P/S)   Activity: Family Members
(T/P)   Improvisation: Hansel & Gretel
(P/S)   Song: The More We Sign Together
(T)   Activity: Color letter of the week page in the activity guide
(P/S)   Activity: Complete letter of the week pages in the activity guide

(I/T/P)   Story: <u>The Berenstain Bears: We Are A Family</u> by Stan & Jan Berenstain (family)
(I/T/P/S)   Story: <u>Counting Kisses)</u> by Karen Katz (home, family)
Time to Sign Props: Family Tree Poster and Infant Cards

Topic 10 – Greetings

(I)   Learn: Hello, Goodbye, how are you? Fine, and then basic signs go, stop, ball, cat, dog
(T/P)   Learn: Greetings signs - Hello, goodbye, how are you?, fine
(S)   Learn: Greetings signs - Hello, goodbye, how are you?, fine, okay, good morning, good afternoon, good night
(I/T/P)   Song: Where is Thumbkin?
(T/P/S)   Activity: Meet & Greet (ask age appropriate questions)
(T/P/)   Activity: Review letters past letters using review page in activity guide
(S)   Activity: Complete "Mystery Solvers" page in activity guide
(I/T/P/S)   Story: <u>Hello! Good-bye!</u> By Aliki (greetings)
Time to Sign Props: Emotions Poster

Topic 11 - Zoo/Jungle Animals

(I/T)   Learn: Zoo/Jungle Animal signs - Alligator, bear, lion, monkey, elephant
(P/S)   Learn: Zoo/Jungle Animal signs - Alligator, animal, bear, camel, elephant, giraffe, hippopotamus, lion, monkey, panda, penguin, tiger, zebra, zoo, jungle
(T/P/S)   Activity: I'm Going to the Zoo
(T/P)   Song: Five Little Monkeys
(S)   Activity: Circle Call Game - Endangered Species
(T)   Activity: Color the letter of the week page in the activity guide
(P/S)   Activity: Complete letter of the week activities in the activity guide
(I/T)   Story: <u>Peek-a-Boo Zoo</u> by Susan Hood (zoo animals)
(I/T/P/S)   Story: <u>Inside A Zoo in the City</u> by Alyssa Satin Capucilli (zoo animals)
Time to Sign Props: Wee See Jungle Animals Story

Topic 12 – Colors

(I)   Learn: Color signs - red, green, blue, yellow
(T/P/S)   Learn: Color signs - Black, blue, brown, colors, gold, gray, green, orange, pink, purple, rainbow, red, silver, white, yellow
(I/T/P/S)   Song: Colors (Use instrumental-Farmer in the Dell)
(T/P/S)   Activity: I Spy
(T/P/S)   Song/Activity: Color Exercise Activity (in the activity guide)
(T/P)   Activity: Sounds of Rainbow
(S)   Activity: Circle Call Game - Endangered Species with Colors

(T/P)   Song: Make New Friends
(T)   Activity: Color the letter of the week page of the activity guide
(P/S)   Activity: Complete the letter of the week activities in the activity guide
(P/S)   Activity: Complete color match in activity guide
(I/T)   Story: <u>Little Blue & Little Yellow</u> by Leo Lioni (colors, family)
(I/T/P/S) Story: <u>White Rabbit's Color Book</u> by Alan Baker (colors)
Time to Sign Props: Colors and Shapes Poster

Topic 13 – Shapes

(I)   Learn: car, airplane, book, toilet, bath, bed, play
(T)   Learn: Shapes signs - Circle, heart, square, and triangle
(P/S)   Learn: Shapes signs - Circle, diamond, heart, oval, rectangle, shape, square, and triangle
(P/S)   Activity: Body Shapes
(T/P)   Song: Shape Song
(T/P/S)   Play: I Spy (with shapes and colors)
(T)   Activity: Color letter of the week page in the activity guide
(P/S)   Activity: Complete letter of the week and shape activities in the activity guide
(I/T/P/S) Story: <u>Brown Rabbit's Shape Book</u> by Alan Baker (colors, shapes)
Time to Sign Props: Colors and Shapes Posters

Topic 14 - Ocean Animals

(I)   Learn: Ocean Animal signs - Fish, turtle, shark, water
(P/T/S)   Learn: Ocean Animal signs - Fish, sea turtle, shark, starfish, whale, beach, ocean, sand, water
(I/T/P)   Song: I'm a Fish (use instrumental CD- "I'm a Little Teapot")
(P/S)   Activity: Circle Call Game - Ocean Animals
(P/S)   Improvisation: Under the Sea
(T)   Activity: Color letter of the week page in the activity guide
(P/S)   Activity: Complete letter of the week activities in the activity guide
(I/T/P/S) Story: <u>Whales Passing</u> by Eve Bunting (ocean animals)
(I/T/P/S) Story: <u>What's Under the Sea</u> by Janet Craig (ocean animals)
Time to Sign Props: We See Ocean Animals Story

Topic 15 – Foods, Preparing to Eat

(I/T)	Learn: Eat, cup, spoon, and fork
(P/S)	Learn: Preparing to eat signs - fork, napkin, plate, spoon, basket, bowl, cup/glass
(P)	Activity: Harvesting Movements
(T/P)	Song: Wash Your Hands (use instrumental CD - "Row, Row, Row Your Boat")
(T/P)	Song: Clean Up (no music required)
(I/T/P)	Song: I'm A Little Tea Pot (use instrumental)
(S)	Song: Filled up Picnic Basket
(T)	Activity: Review letters past letters
(P)	Activity: Review letters past letters in activity guide
(S)	Activity: Complete "Mystery Solvers" Page in activity guide.
(I/T/P/S)	<u>Pancakes, Pancakes</u> by Eric Carle (foods, utensils)

Time to Sign Props: Healthy Foods Poster

Topic 16 – Foods - General

(I)	Learn: General Foods signs - breakfast, lunch, dinner, snack
(T/P/S)	Learn: General Food signs – breakfast, lunch, dinner, snack, may I?, please, thank you, you're welcome
(P/S)	Activity: Meal Time
(P/S)	Song: Use Your Manners
(P/S)	Activity: Complete "Food Pyramid" page in activity guide
(T)	Activity: Color letter of the week page in the activity guide
(P/S)	Activity: Complete letter of the week activities in the activity guide
(T/P/S)	Song: Please & Thank You
(I/T/P)	Story: How Do Dinosaurs Eat Their Food by Jane Yolen (foods, manners)
(I/T/P/S)	Story: <u>Stone Soup</u> by Ann McGovern, Winslow Pinn Ey Pels (foods)

Time to Sign Props: Healthy Foods Poster

Topic 17 – Foods - Fruits

(I)	Learn: Fruit signs - Fruit, orange, apple, pears, grapes
(T/P/S)	Learn: Fruit signs - Fruit, peach, lemon, strawberry, orange, pear, banana, apple, grapes, peach
(P/S)	Song: Apples & Bananas
(P/S)	Activity: Circle Call Game - Fruits
(T/P/S)	Activity: My Favorite – Fruit
(P/S)	Activity: Complete Fruit activity in the activity guide
(T)	Activity: Color letter of the week page in the activity guide
(P/S)	Activity: Complete the letter of the week activities in the activity guide

(I/T/P/S)   Story: <u>Eating the Alphabet: Fruits & Vegetables from A to Z</u> by Lois Ehlert
                Time to Sign Props: Healthy Foods Poster

Topic 18 – Foods – Fun Foods

(I)   Learn: Milk, crackers, cookies, thirsty
(T/P/S)   Learn: Fun Food Signs - Ice cream, cake, cookies, milk, soda, cheese, crackers, French fries, pizza, chicken, hot dog, macaroni, raisin, hungry, delicious, thirsty
(P/S)   Song: A Filled Up Picnic Basket (To the tune of "A Tisket, a Tasket"- no music provided)
(T/P/S)   Activity: My Favorite - Food
(S)   Activity: Gum Drop Pass
(T/P/S)   Song: If You're Hungry and You Know It
(T)   Activity: Color the letter of the week page in the activity guide
(P/S)   Activity: Complete the letter of the week activities in the activity guide
(I/T/P/S)   Story: <u>The Very Hungry Caterpillar</u> by Eric Carle (insects, days of the week, food)
                Time to Sign Props: Healthy Foods Poster

Topic 19 – Foods - Vegetables

(I)   Learn: Vegetable signs - Carrots, peas, corn, vegetables
(T/P/S)   Learn: Vegetable signs - Vegetable, carrots, peas, broccoli, corn, potato
(S)   Activity: Complete the vegetable cross word in the activity guide
(T/P)   Song: Veggies Song
(T/P/S)   Activity: My Favorite - Vegetable
(P/S)   Song: Pumpkin, Pumpkin (To the "Humpty Dumpty" chant-no music provided)
(T)   Activity: Color the letter of the week page of the activity guide
(P/S)   Activity: Complete the letter of the week activities in the activity guide
(P/S)   Improvisation: The Scarecrow
(I/T/P/S)   Story: <u>Growing Vegetable Soup</u> by Lois Ehlert (farm, garden, and foods)
                Time to Sign Props: Healthy Foods Poster

Topic 20 – Foods - Tastes & Textures

(I/T)   Learn: Hot, cold, soft, sweet, sour, delicious
(P/S)   Learn: Taste & Texture signs (delicious, sour, sweet, hot, cold, hard, soft, rough, smooth, fruits, colors)
(P/S)   Activity: Smelling

(P/S)	Activity: Feely Box
(T/P/S)	Activity: Hot Potato
(T/P)	Song: Muffin Man
(P/S)	Song: Apples & Bananas
(T)	Activity: Review letters past letters
(P)	Activity: Review letters past letters using review page in activity guide
(S)	Activity: Complete "Mystery Solvers" page in activity guide
(I/T/P/S)	Story: <u>Cloudy with a Chance of Meatballs</u> by Judi Barrett (foods, utensils,)

Time to Sign Props: Healthy Foods Poster

Topic 21 – Pets

(I)	Learn: Pet signs - Dog, cat, fish, bird
(T/P/S)	Learn: Pet signs - Dog, cat, horse, frog, turtle, mouse, rabbit, snake, bird, fish
(T/P)	Activity: Wing Warm Up - As a Bird
(T/P/S)	Song: Where Are My Pets?
(S)	Activity: Circle Call Game - Pets
(P/S)	Song: Ten Little Bunnies (use instrumental CD- "Ten Little Indians")
(T/P/S)	Activity: My Favorite – Pet
(T)	Activity: Color letter of the week page of the activity guide
(P/S)	Activity: Complete letter of the week activities in the activity guide
(S)	Activity: Complete Pet match up in activity guide
(I/T/P/S)	Story: <u>The Tale of Peter Rabbit</u> by Beatrix Potter (animals)

Time to Sign Props: We See Pet Animals

Topic 22 – Day Signs

(I)	Learn: Time signs - Now, night, morning, day
(T)	Learn: Time signs – Day, night, morning, yesterday, today, and tomorrow
(P/S)	Learn: Days of the Week signs - Day, week, yesterday, today, and tomorrow, Monday, Tuesday, Wednesday, Thursday, Friday, Saturday, and Sunday
(T/P/S)	Song: Seven Days in a Week
(T/P/S)	Activity: My Favorite – Day
(P/S)	Activity: Complete calendar pages in the activity guide
(T/P/S)	Activity: Review the activity calendar for the daily activities
(T)	Activity: Color letter of the week page in the activity guide
(P/S)	Activity: Complete the letter of the week activities in the activity guide
(I/T/P/S)	Story: <u>Today is Monday</u> by Eric Carle (days of the week)

Time to Sign Props: My First Songs in Sign with Spanish Music Book and CD, Activity Clock and Activities

Topic 23 – Naptime & Bedtime

(I)	Learn: Bedtime signs - Bottle, sleep, blanket, diaper, milk
(T/P)	Learn: Bedtime signs - Blanket, pillow, bottle, milk, water, sleep, teddy bear, diaper, potty, brush teeth, light
(S)	Learn: Bedtime signs - blanket, pillow, milk, water, sleep, teddy bear, bathroom, clean, brush teeth, light
(T/P/S)	Song/Activity: Teddy Bear, Teddy Bear (use own tune-no music provided)
(T/P)	Song: Twinkle, Twinkle Little Star
(T/P/S)	Song: Five Little Monkeys
(T)	Activity: look at activity calendar and discuss times to nap and sleep
(P/S)	Activity: Discuss nightly activities before bed (brush teeth, bath, story...)
(T)	Activity: Color letter of the week page in the activity guide
(P/S)	Activity: Complete letter of the week activities in the activity guide
(I/T/P/S)	Story: <u>Good Night Moon</u> by Margaret Wise (home, night)
(I/T/P/S)	Story: <u>How do Dinosaurs Say Good Night</u> by Jane Yolen (home, sleep)

Props: Wee See Stories for reading at bed time; Garlic Press Board Book Home, Play

Topic 24 – Bath Time

(I/T)	Learn: Water, cold, hot, wet, dry, clean
(P/S)	Learn: Bath Time signs - Water, hot, cold, wet, dry, duck, fish, shark, clean, soap, play, fun
(T/P)	Activity: Water, Water Everywhere
(I/T/P)	Song: Row, Row, Row Your Boat
(T/P)	Song: I'm a Fish (use instrumental CD- "I'm a Little Teapot")
(P/S)	Song: Six Little Ducks
(P/S)	Activity: Under the Sea
(T)	Activity: Color letter of the week page in the activity guide
(P/S)	Activity: Complete letter of the week activities in the activity guide
(I/T/P/S)	Story: <u>The Pain and the Great One</u> by Judy Blume (family, bath)

Props: Garlic Press Board Books: Play Signs, Home Signs

Topic 25 – Community - General

(I/T)	Learn: Community signs – Friend, toy, book, read
(P/S)	Learn: Community signs - Friend, neighbor, library, book, quiet, read, playground, restaurant, school, store, toy
(T/P)	Song: We've Been Playing
(P/S)	Song: School Bus
(T/P/S)	Song: What is My Job? (use Instrumental CD - "Where's Thumbkin?")

(T/P)	Improvisation: The Toy Store
(T)	Activity: Review letters past letters using the activity guide
(P)	Activity: Review letters past letters using activity guide
(S)	Activity: When I grow up I want to be...
(I/T/P/S)	Story: <u>Community Helpers from A to Z</u> by Bobbie Kalman (community)

Topic 26 – Community - Fire

(I)	Learn: Help, hurt, safe, need
(T/P/S)	Learn: Fire signs - Ambulance, firefighter, fire engine, help, hurt, safety, 9-1-1
(T/P/S)	Activity: Fire Drill
(T/P/S)	Activity: Smoke Crawl
(I/T/P/S)	Song: I'm a Firefighter
(T/P)	Activity: Badge - Fire
(T)	Activity: Color letter of the week page in the activity guide
(P/S)	Activity: Complete letter of the week activities in the activity guide
(I/T/P/S)	Story: <u>Fireman Small</u> by Wong Herbert Lee (community fire)

Topic 27 – Community - Police

(I/T)	Learn: police office, police car
(T/P/S)	Learn Police signs - Safety, police officer, traffic light, help, police car, 9-1-1
(T/P)	Activity: Badge - Police
(I/T/P)	Song: I'm a Police Officer
(P/S)	Song: Buckle Bear Safety Song
(T/P)	Song: Traffic Light
(P/S)	Song: Safety Belts (to the tune of "Jingle Bells"-no music provided)
(T)	Activity: Color letter of the week page in the activity guide
(P/S)	Activity: Complete letter of the week activities in the activity guide
(I/T/P/S)	Story: <u>Office Buckle and Gloria</u> by Peggy Rathmann (community, police)

Topic 28 – Community – Post Office

(I/T/P/S)	Learn: Postal signs - Address, box, letter/mail, mailbox, mail carrier, post office, stamp, write
(T/P)	Activity: Letter Warm Up
(I/T/P/S)	Song: I'm a Little Letter (use instrumental CD- "I'm a Little Teapot")
(T)	Activity: Color letter of the week page in the activity guide
(P/S)	Activity: Complete letter of the week activities in the activity guide
(T/P/S)	Learn: *(Review)* – Hello, goodbye, how are you?, okay, fine, wonderful/terrific
(I/T/P/S)	Story: <u>A Letter to Amy</u> by Jack Keats (mail, friends)

Topic 29 – Community - Health

(I/T)	Learn: Health Care signs – earache, belly ache, feel, hurt/pain
(P/S)	Learn: Health Care signs - Body, 9-1-1, dentist, doctor, earache, feel, hospital, hurt, nurse, sick, brush hair, brush teeth, teeth
(I/T/P)	Song: My Dentist (use Instrumental CD- "Where's Thumbkin?")
(T/P/S)	Song: Five Little Monkeys
(T/P)	Song: Mulberry Bush
(T/P/S)	Review: hand washing with fun soap
(S)	Activity: Complete emergency signs page in the activity guide
(T)	Activity: Color letter of the week page in the activity guide
(P/S)	Activity: Complete letter of the week activities in the activity guide
(I/T/P/S)	Story: Farm Flu by Teresa Bateman (community, health)

Topic 30 – Community - Construction

(I)	Learn: *(Review)* – Mom, dad, please, thank you, good
(T/P/S)	Learn: Construction signs - Build, dirt, move, tools, truck
(T/P)	Activity: Front End Loader
(P/S)	Activity: Build a Bridge
(P/S)	Song: London Bridge
(T/P/S)	Review: past letters using activity guide
(I/T/P/S)	Story: Family and Community by Jane Schneider (community, construction)

Topic 31 – Transportation – Car

(I)	Learn: Transportation signs – Airplane, car, fly, boat
(T/P/S)	Learn: Transportation signs - Airplane, bridge, bus, car, fly, racing, ride, row boat, street, wheels, wipers
(T/P)	Activity: Travel Starter
(T/P/S)	Song: Car Song
(I/T/P)	Song: Windshield Wiper (use Instrumental CD- "I'm a Little Teapot")
(P/S)	Song: The Transportation Song
(T)	Activity: Color letter of the week page in the activity guide
(P/S)	Activity: Complete letter of the week activities in the activity guide
(I/T/P/S)	Story: Little Bear by Else Holmelund Minarik (family, transportation, car)

Props: Numbers to Transportation Cards

Topic 32 – Transportation – General

(I)	Learn: Transportation signs- *(Review)* Airplane, car, fly, boat
(T/P/S)	Learn: Transportation signs - Airplane, bicycle, bus, car, horse, skateboard, sled, truck, walk
(T/P)	Activity: Body Wheels
(T/P/S)	Song: Over the River and Through the Woods
(I/T/P/S)	Song: Wheels on the Bus
(T/P)	Song: School Bus
(T)	Activity: Color letter of the week page in the activity guide
(P/S)	Activity: Complete letter of the week activities in the activity guide
(I/T/P/S)	Story: <u>The Wheels on the Bus and Other Transportation Songs</u> by Scholastic, Illustrated by Dick Witt (transportation general)

Time to Sign Props: Numbers to Transportation Cards

Topic 33 – Transportation – Trains

(I/T/P/S)	Learn: Transportation signs – train, track, airplane, bicycle, bus, car, horse, skateboard, sled, train, truck, walk
(T/P)	Activity: Toddler Train
(T/P)	Activity: Ride the Rails
(T/P/S)	Song: She'll Be Coming Around the Mountain
(T/P)	Song: I've Been Working on the Railroad
(T/P/S)	Activity: Review Alphabet; finger spell names
(I/T/P/S)	Story: <u>The Little Engine that Could</u> by Watty Piper (transportation, train)

Time to Sign Props: Numbers to Transportation Cards

Topic 34 – Transportation – Safety

(I)	Learn: *(Review)* - Apple, banana, cookie, milk, help
(T/P/S)	Learn: Transportation signs - Ambulance, buckle, fire engine, seat belt, stop sign, traffic light, wipers
(T/P)	Activities: Roly Poly Races
(T)	Activity: Color letter of the week page in the activity guide
(P/S)	Activity: Complete letter of the week activities in the activity guide
(T/P)	Song: Buckle Bear Safety Song
(T/P)	Song Traffic Light
(I/T/P)	Song: Windshield Wiper (use Instrumental CD- "I'm a Little Teapot")
(I/T/P/S)	Story: <u>I Fly</u> by Anne Rockwell (transportation)

Time to Sign Props: Numbers to Transportation Cards

Topic 35 – Transportation – Water

(I)	Learn: *(Review)* – Boat, pig, sheep, dog, cat, horse
(T/P/S)	Learn: Transportation -Water signs - Boat, bridge, row boat, sailboat
(T/P)	Activity: Travel Starter
(T/P)	Activity: Boat Adventure
(T)	Activity: Color letter of the week page in the activity guide
(P/S)	Activity: Complete letter of the week activities in the activity guide
(T/P)	Song: Row, Row, Row Your Boat
(T/P/S)	Song: Down by the Station
(I/T/P/S)	Story: Row, Row, Row Your Boat by Iza Trapani (transportation)

*Time to Sign Props: Numbers to Transportation Cards, We See Ocean Animals Story

Topic 36 – Nature

(I)	Learn: Nature signs – Green, outside, grass, tree, sun
(T/P/S)	Learn: Nature signs - Forest, grass, lake, moon, mountain, ocean, outside, path/trail, river, sand, sky, stars, sun, tree, world
(I/T/P)	Song: Mulberry Bush
(P/S)	Song: Tell Me Why?
(I/T)	Song: The Bear Went Over the Mountain
(T)	Activity: Color letter of the week page in the activity guide
(P/S)	Activity: Complete letter of the week activities in the activity guide
(I/T/P/S)	Activity: Nature walk with sign language
(S)	Activity: Complete hidden picture activity in activity guide
(I/T/P/S)	Story: Someday a Tree by Eve Bunting (nature)

Topic 37 – Nature 2

(I/)	Learn: *(Review)* - Green, outside, grass, tree, sun
(T/P/S)	Learn: *(Review)* - Nature signs - Forest, grass, lake, moon, mountain, ocean, outside, path/trail, river, sand, sky, stars, sun, tree, world
(T/P)	Activity: Nature Warm Up
(T)	Activity: Color letter of the week page in the activity guide
(P/S)	Activity: Complete letter of the week activities in the activity guide
(I/T/P)	Poem: Way Up High in the Apple Tree
(T/P)	Song: Twinkle, Twinkle Little Star
(T/P/S)	Song: Mr. Sun
(I/T/P/S)	Story: The Season's of Arnold's Apple Tree by Gail Gibbons (nature)

Topic 38 – Science & Nature - Bugs

(I)   Learn: Bug/Insect signs - Bug, spider, worm, butterfly
(T/P/S)   Learn: Bug/Insect signs - Ant, bee, bug, butterfly, firefly, ladybug, spider, worm
(T/P)   Activity: Beehive
(T)   Activity: Color letter of the week page in the activity guide
(P/S)   Activity: Complete letter of the week activities in the activity guide
(T/P/S)   Song: Bumble Bee
(T/P)   Dance: Dance of the Honeybees
(T/P/S)   Song: The Ants Go Marching – Use age appropriate signs
(I/T/P/S)   Story: <u>The Grouchy Ladybug</u> by Eric Carle (nature, bugs)
Time to Sign Props: We See Bugs Story

Topic 39 – Science & Nature - Bugs

(I)   Learn: *(Review)* - Bug, spider, worm, butterfly
(T/P/S)   Learn: Bug/Insect signs - Ant, bee, bug, butterfly, firefly, ladybug, spider, worm
(T/P)   Activity: Caterpillar Warm Up
(T/P)   Activity: The Butterfly Story
(T)   Activity: Color letter of the week page in the activity guide
(P/S)   Activity: Complete letter of the week activities in the activity guide
(T/P/S)   Song: Flutter, Flutter Butterfly (to the tune of "Twinkle, Twinkle, Little Star"-no music provided)
(I/T/P/S)   Song: Itsy-Bitsy Spider
(I/T/P/S)   Story: <u>Itsy Bitsy Spider</u>, by various authors (bugs, spider)
Time to Sign Props: We See Bugs Story

Topic 40 – Science & Nature - Weather

(I/T)   Learn: Weather signs – Cold, hot, sun, rain, wind, snow
(P/S)   Learn: Weather signs (cold, clouds, hot, lightning, rain, rainbow, snow, storm, sun, thunder, warm, weather, wind)
(T/P)   Activity: Clouds in the Breeze
(T/P)   Activity: Mighty Wind
(T)   Activity: Color letter of the week page in the activity guide
(P/S)   Activity: Complete letter of the week activities in the activity guide
(T/P/S)   Song: What will the Weather be?
(T/P)   Activity: Boat Adventure
(I/T/P)   Song: Rain, Rain Go Away (use Instrumental CD-"Row, Row, Row your Boat-Slow)
(P/S)   Song: Mr. Sun
(I/T/P/S)   <u>Little Cloud</u> by Eric Carle (weather)
Time to Sign Props: Weather Poster

Topic 41 – Science & Nature – Weather 2

(I)	Learn: Weather signs – *(Review)* Cold, hot, sun, rain, wind, snow
(T/P/S)	Learn: Weather signs – *(Review)* - Cold, clouds, hot, lightning, rain, rainbow, snow, storm, sun, thunder, warm, weather, wind
(T/P)	Activity: Storm Winds
(T)	Activity: Color letter of the week page in the activity guide
(P/S)	Activity: Complete letter of the week activities in the activity guide
(T/P)	Song: Itsy bitsy Spider
(I/T/P)	Song: The Weather Song (to the tune of "Clementine"-no music provided)
(I/P/S)	Song: You Are My Sunshine
(T/P)	Song: What Will the Weather Be?
(I/T/P/S)	The Mitten by Jan Brett (seasons, weather)

**Time to Sign Props: Weather Poster

Topic 42 – Science & Nature – Winter Burr

(I)	Learn: Winter signs - Cold, winter, blanket, outside
(T/P/S)	Learn: Winter signs - Cold, sled/sleigh, snow, white, winter
(T/P)	Activity: Snow Ball Starter
(T/P)	Activity: Melt Down
(T)	Activity: Color letter of the week page in the activity guide
(P/S)	Activity: Complete letter of the week activities in the activity guide
(P/S)	Song: She'll Be Coming Around the Mountain
(T/P/S)	Song: Over the River and Through the Woods
(I/T/P/S)	The Snowy Day by Ezra Jack Keats (weather)

**Time to Sign Props: Weather Poster

Topic 43 – Science & Nature – Summer Fun

(I)	Learn: Summer signs - Game, hot, play, warm, tree
(T/P/S)	Learn: Summer signs - Beach, camping, fireworks, game, hot, picnic, play, river, summer time, sun, tree, warm, water
(T/P)	Activity: Water, Water Everywhere
(T/P/S)	Activity: Crossing the River
(T)	Activity: Color letter of the week page in the activity guide
(P/S)	Activity: Complete letter of the week activities in the activity guide
(T/P/S)	Song: It's Summer Time Again
(T/P/S)	Song: Mr. Sun
(T/P/S)	Song: You Are My Sunshine
(T/P)	Improvisation: My Day in the a Park
(I/T/P/S)	Story: The Season's of Arnold's Apple Tree by Gail Gibbons (nature)

*Time to Sign Props: Weather Poster

Topic 44 – General - Bubbles

(I)	Learn: Bubble signs - Bubble, down, me, wind
(T/P/S)	Learn: Bubble signs - Bubble, down, dry, me/I, round, shiny, wind
(T/P/S)	Activity: Beautiful Bubble
(T/P/S)	Activity: My Bubble
(T)	Activity: Color letter of the week page in the activity guide
(P/S)	Activity: Complete letter of the week activities in the activity guide
(T/P/S)	Song: I'm a Little Bubble (use Instrumental CD- "I'm a Little Teapot")
(I/T/P/S)	Story: Bubble Ridding a Relaxation Story by Lori Lite

Topic 45 – General - Clothing

(I)	Learn: Clothing signs - Hat, shoes, socks, shirt
(T/P/S)	Learn: Clothing signs - Dress, hat, pants, scarf, shirt, shoes, socks, sweater
(P/S)	Activity: Scarf Starter
(T/P/S)	Activity: My Bare Feet
(T/P/S)	Activity: Wonder Shoes
(T)	Activity: Color letter of the week page in the activity guide
(P/S)	Activity: Complete letter of the week activities in the activity guide
(T/P/S)	Song: Shirts, Pants, Shoes & Socks (to the tune of "Head, Shoulders, Knees and Toes"-no music provided)
(I/T/P/S)	Story: All by Myself by Aliki (clothing)

Topic 46 – General - Sizes

(I)	Learn: Size signs - Big, little
(T/P/S)	Learn: Size signs - Big, little, tall, short, long
(T/P/S)	Activity: Who Is the Biggest?
(T/P)	Activity: Tall or Short
(T)	Activity: Color letter of the week page in the activity guide
(P/S)	Activity: Complete letter of the week activities in the activity guide
(I/T/P)	Song: I'm a Little Teapot
(T/P/S)	Song: I'm a Little Bubble (use Instrumental CD- "I'm a Little Teapot")
(T/P/S)	Song: Six Little Ducks
(I/T/P/S)	Story: Tall by Jez Alborough

Topic 47 – Garden – Flower, Garden

(I/T)	Learn: Flower and Garden signs – Flower, grow, fruit, vegetables sun
(P/S)	Learn: Flower & Garden signs - Flower, garden, grow, food, hay, fruits, vegetables, dirt, rain, sun, hoe, plants, seeds, shovel
(T/P/S)	Activity: Flower Warm Up
(T/P)	Activity: Flower Garden
(T)	Activity: Color letter of the week page in the activity guide
(P/S)	Activity: Complete letter of the week activities in the activity guide
(I/T/P/S)	Song: I'm A Little Flower (use Instrumental CD- "I'm a Little Teapot")
(T/P/S)	Improvisation: Jack and the Beanstalk
(T/P)	Song: Veggies Song
(T/P)	Song: Fruit Song
(I/T/P/S)	Story: The Tiny Seed by Eric Carle (garden)
	Time to Sign Prop: Healthy Foods Poster

Topic 48 – Sports & Recreation - Camping

(I)	Learn: camp, fish, field
(T/P/S)	Learn: Camping signs - Camping, backpacking, climbing, field, fishing, horseback riding, path/trail, rock climbing, sailing, swimming, walk
(T/P/S)	Activity: Camp In
(T)	Activity: Color letter of the week page in the activity guide
(P/S)	Activity: Complete letter of the week activities in the activity guide
(T/P/S)	Song: Camping Song (use Instrumental CD- "Where's Thumbkin?")
(T/P)	Song: March & Sing (to the tune of "Mulberry Bush")-no music provided
(I/T/P/S)	Story: Curious George Goes Camping by H.A. Rey

Topic 49 – Sports & Recreation – Sports

(I)	Learn: Sports signs – Ball, throw, play, outside
(T/P/S)	Learn: Sports signs - Ball, basketball, catch, dodge ball, football, golf, throw
(T/P)	Activity: Be the Bouncing Ball
(P/S)	Activity: Basketball (Nerf)
(P/S)	Activity: Dodge Ball (Nerf)
(P/S)	Activity: Football (Nerf)
(T/P/S)	Activity: Golf (putting)
(T)	Activity: Color letter of the week page in the activity guide
(P/S)	Activity: Complete letter of the week activities in the activity guide
(T/P/S)	Song: It's Summer Time Again
(I/T/P/S)	Story: Froggy Plays T-Ball by Jonathan London (sports, baseball)

Topic 50 – Sports & Recreation – Sports 2

(I)	Learn: Sports signs – *(Review)* - Ball, throw, play, outside
(T/P/S)	Learn: Sports signs - Ball, catch, gymnastics, ice skating, soccer, swimming, throw, volleyball
(T/P)	Activity: Be the Bouncing Ball
(T/P/S)	Activity: Gymnastics (tumbling)
(T/P/S)	Activity: Ice Skating (in socks)
(T/P/S)	Activity: Soccer (kick, Nerf)
(T/P/S)	Activity: Swimming (strokes in air, swim on floor)
(P/S)	Activity: Volleyball (balloon or beach ball volleyball)
(T)	Activity: Color letter of the week page in the activity guide
(P/S)	Activity: Complete letter of the week activities in the activity guide
(I/T/P/S)	Story: <u>Franklin Plays the Game</u> by Paulette Bourgeois (sports)

Topic 51 – Sports, Recreation & Arts - Arts

(I)	Learn: Art signs – colors, dance, drum, music
(T/P/S)	Learn: Art signs - Acting, art, band, basket, camera, colors, dance, draw, drum, guitar, music, paint, puppets, violin, xylophone
(T/P)	Activity: Leonardo's Warm Up
(P/S)	Song: Color Song
(I/T/P/S)	Song: Colors (Use instrumental-Farmer in the Dell)
(T/P)	Activity: Air Band
(T)	Activity: Color letter of the week page in the activity guide
(P/S)	Activity: Complete letter of the week activities in the activity guide
(I/T/P/S)	Story: <u>Angelina Ballerina</u> by Katharine Holabird (fine & arts)

Topic 52 – Sports, Recreation & Arts – Movement Songs

(I/T/P/S)	Learn: Jump, Move, Dance, Music
(I/T/P/S)	Activity: Jumping Beans
(T/P/S)	Song: Five Little Monkeys
(T/P/S)	Activity: Pattern Formation
(T)	Activity: Color letter of the week page in the activity guide
(P/S)	Activity: Complete letter of the week activities in the activity guide
(P/S)	Song: The Ants Go Marching In
(T/P)	Song: Itsy-Bitsy Spider
(T/P)	Song: March & Sing (to the tune of "Mulberry Bush")-no music provided
(T/P/S)	Song Music: Touch Your Nose (use own tune-no music provided)
(T/P/S)	Song: Head, Shoulders, Knees and Toes (use it's tune-no music provided)

Topic 53 – Months

Handouts for months of the year go home the first week of each month

(P/S)

January	May	September
February	June	October
March	July	November
April	August	December

(I/T) Learn: Previous signs – Choose previous topic signs that were most efficient for your children

(P/S) Recap: Month Signs (each day of each month you meet)

(T/P/S) Use activity guide activities on calendar.

Topic 54 – Holidays

Handouts for holidays go home throughout the year as appropriate

(I/T/P/S) **Birthday**
Song: Happy Birthday (no music provided)

Christmas
Activity: Reindeer Dance
Song: Jingle Bells (no music provided)
Song: We Wish You A Merry Christmas (no music provided)

Easter
Song: A Filled Up Picnic Basket (use tune of "A Tisket, a Tasket"- no music provided)

Halloween
Song: Five Little Pumpkins (use tune of "Five Little Monkeys"-no music provided)
Song: Jack-O-Lantern (use Instrumental CD- "I'm a Little Teapot")
Song Music: Pumpkin, Pumpkin (to the chant of "Humpty, Dumpty"-no music provided)
Improvisation: Halloween

Hanukkah
Song: Eight Little Candles (to the tune of "Twinkle, Twinkle, Little Star"-no music provided)
Song: I'm A Little Dreidel (use tune to "I'm a Little Teapot")

Independence Day - July 4th
Songs: Stars & Stripes (use tune to - "Row, Row, Row Your Boat")

Kwanzaa
Song: Kwanzaa's Here (to the tune of "Three Blind Mice")

Thanksgiving
Song: (use tune to Over the River and Through the Woods)

Valentine's Day
Song: I'm A Little Valentine (use tune to "I'm a Little Teapot")

Mother's Day
Song: Happy Mother's Day (use own tune)

Father's Day
Song: Happy Father's Day (use own tune)

*Props: Use Handouts, other propos to purchase Sign Language Holidays and Celebrations book (Garlic Press Co.)

CHAPTER 9:
SIGN LANGUAGE ACTIVITIES

PLAYING WITH OTHERS IS
A GREAT WAY TO LEARN!

Activities

Air Band
Warm up exercise. Have the children mimic the playing of various band instruments.
Play rhythmic music in the background. Below are some suggestions to get you started:
    Have your children pretend to play the xylophone
    Then have them play a violin
    Then have them play a guitar
    Then have them play a stand up base
    Then have them play the drums
    Then have them play the keyboards
    End with them playing whatever instrument they choose

Teach children signs for music and instruments.

ABC Animals
Sit in a circle. Teacher begins by using ABC Animal cards and teaching the children all the alphabet animals. The teacher shows the animal sign for all the children to see. The teacher begins the game by placing all the alphabet number cards in the middle of the circle, then the teacher points to each child (one at a time) and ask to find an animal or letter in the middle by doing the animal sign (example, doing the monkey sign) and then the child must find the animal shown by the teacher by going through the animal cards in the middle. Once the child has found the correct animal then the child places the animal card in front of them so that other children can see the animal sign and to continue playing the game.. The teacher continues until all children have a different animal card in front of them in the circle. To continue the game the teacher then begins by teaching the children the put back sign and explains to the children that she will do the put back sign and animal sign and then child who has the animal card must place the animal card back into the middle of the circle. This continues until all cards are back to the middle of the circle.

Animal Hop
Stand in a circle. Teach the children the signs for different animals (farm, zoo, ocean, insects) and how they hop. Play some lively music in the background and have them hop around imitating the animals. Do not tell them the animals to become, rather just use the signs to show them what they are to be next.

Teach children signs for animals.

Badge - Fire or Police
Supply the children with tag board in the shape of a badge. Have them wrap tin foil around the badge to make a police badge.

Materials: tag board, aluminum foil.

Teach children signs for Firefighter, Police Officer, badge.

Be the Bouncing Ball
Have the children pretend they have eaten a rubber bouncing ball by mistake. They thought it was a gumball. As the ball moves into different parts of their bodies those parts bounce up and down.

First their heads
Then their shoulders
Then their arms
Then their legs
Then their whole bodies
Finally the ball bounces back out and they cover their mouth.

Teach children signs for ball, body parts, up, down.

Basketball (Nerf)
Stand in a circle. Have the children mimic the following moves.

Pass the ball
Dribble the ball
Shoot the ball

Now introduce the Nerf ball.

Bounce pass the ball to everyone
Everyone dribble the ball once and then pass
Have them take turns shooting at a spot on the floor, taped off

Teach children signs for basketball, ball, pass.

Body Letters
Have the children form the letters with their bodies. Have them form the first letter of the names of all of the children in the classroom. Take pictures so that in the next class you can show them how they look like the letters.

Teach children signs for the letters of the alphabet.

Body Wheels
Warm up exercise. Discover how many different ways your children can make wheels with their bodies. Curl up in a ball, roll sideways, etc.

Have the children turn in a circle.
Have them rotate their arms.
Have them gently rotate their heads.
Have them move their hips.
Have them roll on the floor.

Teach children signs for wheel, circle, gently, move, head.

Beautiful Bubbles

Sit in a circle. Have them watch the bubbles to see how they float on the air. Use a hula hoop as your gigantic magic bubble wand. Have the children step through the hoop and be transformed into giant bubbles. Tell them which way the wind blows and have them move accordingly. Finally they gently rest on the ground curled up in a ball when suddenly they pop, lying flat on the ground.

Teach children signs for bubbles, magic, gigantic (big).

Beehive

Warm up exercise. As the queen bee you will guide your honeybees through their daily activities. Have them mimic the movements you do.
> First have them stretch their wings before flight
> Then have them take off to get the nectar from the flowers, tell them where to go
> Then have them return with the nectar and put it all together in a pot (have them cup their hands full of nectar and carry it back to the pot)
> Have them clean their hands of the sticky stuff

Teach children signs for bee, fly, flowers, pot, clean up.

Boat Adventure

Imagination play activity. Create a boat (this could be an outline on the floor, chairs, or a box). Have the children climb aboard the boat. Pretend you're on a journey to an island far, far away.
> Have them row the boat across the ocean to the island.
> (Talk about the water creatures you saw on the way, as they row. Look it's a whale, look over there it's a shark, etc.)
> The weather gets bad, hold on. (There is rain, wind, lightning, thunder.)
> When they arrive they mimic your actions as they explore the island.
> (You find sand, water, trees, grass, rocks.)
> They pretend to eat their fill of bananas and bring some in a sack for the trip home.
> Off home they row, promising to return some day.

Teach children signs for nature/outdoor signs, weather signs, journey, ocean animals.

Build a Bridge
Sit in a circle. Teach the children the various construction signs such as: build, dig, tractor, tools, move/relocate and truck. Have the children make a human bridge to help replace the one in London that keeps falling down.

Teach children signs for bridge, tractor, truck, build, dig.

Butterfly Metamorphosis
Have the children mimic the movements as you explain the cycle.
     Have the children wiggle on the ground as if they were a caterpillar
     Then have them curl up in a cocoon
     Have them open up their cocoon and step outside
     Have them walk along the branch
     Have them fly
     Have them land again

Teach children signs for butterfly, caterpillar, branch, fly.

Camp In
Set up a tent and create a fake fire out of colored construction paper (the tent can be simply a blanket over chairs). Have the children enter the room and sit around the fire. Talk about all the different things you might see on a camp out. Have the children mimic being the items such as a tree, grass, ground/dirt, water, rain, animals. This is an introduction to camping songs and other activities.

Teach children signs for outdoor/nature, animals.

Cat Warm Up
Stand in a circle. Teach them the sign for cat. Stretch and move as if they were a cat:
     Walk like a cat.
     Curl up to sleep.
     Jump like a cat.
     Pretend to play with a ball of string.
     Pretend to be a cat that is angry or afraid.

Teach children signs for cat, sleep, jump, ball, string, angry, afraid.

Caterpillar Warm Up
Play rhythmic music in the background. Have the children line up in a straight line. Then have them stand on their knees. Have them place their hands upon the shoulders of the person in front of them. Know have them inch forward in unison. Everybody move your right leg (point, show mirroring). Now everybody left, right, left… Have them travel around the room a bit then stop.

Teach children signs for caterpillar.

Circle Call Game

Sit in a circle. One at a time, going around the circle, each child chooses an animal (or color, shape, food, etc.) to sign. The teacher/child shows the animal sign for all the children to see. The teacher begins the game by making her/his animal sign, followed by that of another animal in the circle. It then becomes the turn of the child whose animal sign has been displayed. The child then makes their sign, followed by that of another child. The game continues until all the signs have been learned. It takes approximately 5 minutes for all the signs to be learned. Discuss each animal's habitat, foods, etc.

Add colors to whatever else you are signing. With animals, shapes, foods, etc. just sign both the item or it's name and its color.

Teach children signs for circle, animals, foods, colors, shapes.

Clouds in the Breeze

Tie 12 - 18" long pieces of cloth on the arms of two of the children. All the other children are clouds. The wind will guide the clouds gently around the room. Play some rhythmic music. As the music gets faster so should the wind and the clouds, as the music slows, so should the wind and the clouds.

Teach children signs for cloud, wind, room.

Counting Clothes

Sit or stand in a circle. Teach the children the numbers from 1-10 in sign. Have them use their sign language to count the following:

  How many people are in the circle?
  How many shoes do they have?
  How many socks do they have?
  How many people are wearing blue?
  How many are wearing red?
  How many people are wearing shirts in the circle?
  How many people are wearing pants in the circle?
  How many people are wearing dresses in the circle?

Teach children signs for clothing, colors.

Crossing the River

Sit in a circle. Have the children describe ways in which they would cross a river. Have them mimic the actions it would take to cross the river.

  They could row across in a boat
  They could swim across
  They could jump across
  They could fly over the river in a plane

Teach children signs for river, jump, swim, boat, fly, plane.

Dance of the Honeybees

Explain how bees dance to communicate. Have one little explorer bee buzzing around to the other side of the room and find a beautiful sun flower. Then she returns to the hive to tell the others about what she has found. She does a flying dance to explain what she has found and how to get their. They all buzz over to the sun flower. They then buzz to the lake to get a drink. Then to the park to play. Then home to their hive. Sign the names of common items they may see on their way: nature, park, playground.

Teach children signs for bee, dance, communicate/talk, beautiful, sun, flower, fly, nature, outdoor, park, playground.

Dodge Ball (Nerf)

Have the children play this game on their knees, except to go far to get the ball. Have the group split into two teams. Each time a person gets hit, without catching the ball then she is out. Once out the person moves to the side and assist with retrieving the ball for her teammate(s).

Freeze Dodge Ball: have them stay still in place when hit.

Teach children signs for ball, hit, catch, team.

Duck Relay

Divide the children using their sign language. One team can be the brown ducks and a second the white. Have the children waddle, squatted down, to a point on the floor where a feather lies. Have the child pick it up and return to the point as which she started and hand the feather to the next person in line. They have to follow the same path and pass the feather to the next person (you may wish to also use a cone for them to go around).

Teach children signs for colors, duck, feather.

Family Members

Sit in a circle. Teach the children the different family member signs. Have them each take a turn to tell and sign their immediate family members that live in their home. Talk about other family members who live elsewhere, reiterating the signs as you go. Next week have them bring in a picture of their families and sign their mother, father, brother, sister, etc.

Teach children signs for family members, mother, father, brother, sister, grandmother, grandfather, aunt, uncle, cousin.

Favorite Animal Initials

Sit in a circle. Have each of the children tell you the name of their favorite animal. Help them to form the finger alphabet letter o the first letter of the animal name. You can bring in stuffed animals, beanies or pictures to help.

Teach children signs for animals.

Feely Box
Create feely boxes out of shoe boxes with various food items inside. Cut a hole in the top and tape the side, so it does not open. You can use spaghetti, grapes, crushed cookies or crackers, crushed tomatoes, food colored mashed potatoes, etc.

Sit in a circle. Place the 1st feely box in the middle of the circle. Have each child take a turn putting his/her hand into the feely box and feeling what is inside. Talk about the texture, teaching texture signs as you go. Let them guess what is in the box. Show them what is actually in the box. Create as many feely boxes as you can for each different texture you wish to teach. Give each child a paper towel to clean their hand during the game.

Teach children signs for foods.

Fingerspell First Letter of Children's Names
Sit in a circle. Have each of the children tell you their names. Help them to form the finger alphabet letter for the first letter of their name.

Teach children signs for the letters of the alphabet.

Fire Drill
Sit in a circle. Teach children the sign for fire. Teach them what to do in case there is a fire, or fire alarm, in the building. Have them quietly line up at the door, holding hands. When the teacher opens the door they can then all proceed together down the hall to the nearest designated fire exit and outside. Once outside they continue to their designated spot until the teacher says they can all go bask inside. At which time they all proceed in through the main entrance, holding hands, as a group/in line.

Tell children it is very important that nobody gets left behind. If they know someone is not with the group they need to let the teacher know immediately. Reinforce they will not be in any trouble for telling the teacher, rather they will be a hero.

Teach children signs for fire, room, outside.

Flower Garden
Warm up exercise. Ask them each what color flowers they would like to plant. Then have the children mimic the movements they would make while working in the garden.
> Have them first dig the bed for the flowers
> Have them till the ground with the plow (holding each others feet in the air as they walk slowly along the bed)
> Then have them plant the seeds
> Have them water the flowers (as if a watering can (teapot))
> Have them rake and pull out the weeds
> Now they have created a beautiful garden

Teach children signs for flower, garden, seeds, bed, ground/dirt.

Flower Warm Up

Have the children mimic the following stretches as they imitate a flower:

Have the children curl up tightly in a ball as if they are a flower seed

Have them stand on their knees as they burst out of the ground

Have them stand up with their hands in the air as they grow

Have them bend to the east as the sun arises

Have their hands straight up as the sun is directly overhead

Have them bend to the west as the sun begins to set

Have them return to the straight position as it becomes dark

They then rest for the new day and start all over again

Teach children signs for flower, sun, ball, day, night.

Football (Nerf)

Stand in a circle. Have the children mimic the actions that a football player would make.

Have them pretend to be the quarterback

First they receive the snap

Then they hand the ball off

Then they pass the ball

Have them be the receiver

They run (in place)

Then they catch the ball

Then they run again

Stand in a circle. Pass the ball around the circle. Then underhand toss the ball to each of the children. Have them toss you the ball back.

Teach children signs for football, ball, pass, catch.

Front End Loader

Stand in a circle. Teach the children the various construction signs such as: build, dig, tractor, tools, move/relocate and truck. Have the children mimic the actions of a front end loader as follows:

Dig the dirt

Lift the dirt high in the air

Pour the dirt into the truck

Teach children signs for build, dig, tractor, tools, move/relocate, truck.

Golf

Warm up exercise. Practice swinging the imaginary golf club.

Hit it hard off the tee

Walk to the ball

Hit it medium to approach the flag

Walk to the ball

Put it in the hole

Teach children signs for golf, hard, hit, walk, flag, ball.

Gum Drop Pass
Make 4" colored gum drops (red, green, yellow, orange). Sit in a circle. Give each of the children a clothes pin. Demonstrate how to get the clothespin to open and close. Using the clothespin, pass each of the gum drops around the circle. Send a few around at the same time. Send some the opposite direction. Can also be done as a relay race.

Teach them the sign for colors, candy.

Gymnastics (tumbling)
Use a mat to cushion the children as they tumble. Have rhythmic music playing in the background. Instructor must help guide them as they roll. Be sure the children tuck in their head.

Teach children signs for gymnastics, roll.

Halloween
Have the children mimic you in acting out the actions of the following Halloween creatures with holiday music in the background:
> Ghosts - have the children float around the room.
> Witches - fly on their brooms around the room.
> Skeletons - move around the room as if you are a marionette, controlled by strings.
> Pumpkin - growing bigger and bigger as Halloween approaches.
> Cats - have the children get on all fours and arch their backs up as they walk around the room.

Teach children signs for Halloween, around, room, big, pumpkin, cat.

Hansel & Gretel
Read the children the story. Then teach them the key signs for the story (brother, sister, stop, dance, play, scared, tired, asleep, come on, walk, house, beautiful).
Part 1 - Children take partners becoming Hansel and Gretel. Have them imitate making brooms. Tiring of the work they stop to play and dance (teach them the signs for stop, play, dance; show them how to dance in a circle skipping with arms locked together as a pair). Have them repeat with you the following:
> Brother, come dance with me,
>> Both my hands I offer thee,
> Right foot first, left foot then,
>> Round about and back again.

Part 2 - Children pretend they are taken to the woods. Move them from one side of the room to the other. They become lost (show the signs for scared, tired, sleep), scared, tired and eventually fall asleep (you can play Twinkle, Twinkle Little Star as they pretend to sleep).
Part 3 - Children wake up and see an incredibly beautiful candy house. They then walk towards it, approaching it very carefully.
Part 4 - The evil witch (teacher) beckons then to come in (using words and sign).

Teach children signs for brother, sister, stop, dance, play, scared, tired, asleep, come on, walk, house, beautiful.

Happy or Sad?

Sit in a circle. Give each of the children two paper plates. One with a sad face and one with a happy face. Teach them the signs for happy and sad. Have them choose between happy and sad as you read sentences. With the other hand have them do the sign for happy or sad (these can be done easily with one hand). Some examples are as follows, please feel free to create and use your own.

> I dropped my ice cream on the ground.
> I got a new toy.
> I got to eat my favorite food.
> I got hurt.
> I'm going to the playground.
> I went to go to the doctor.
> I went to the zoo.
> I got to sing my favorite song.
> I got a big lollipop.

Teach children signs for happy, sad, ice cream, toy, food, hurt, playground, doctor, zoo, song.

Harvesting Movements

Stand in a circle. Have the children mimic the movements one would make when harvesting:

> Hoeing - tilling the earth
> Planting - throwing seeds
> Watering - pouring water
> Picking - grabbing and placing in a bag (from above and the ground, apples to potatoes)

Teach children signs for hoe, plant, water, pick.

I'm Going to the Zoo

Sit in a circle. Teach the children various zoo animal signs. Have them take turns signing for you their favorite animal at the zoo.

Teach children signs for zoo animals.

I Spy

Prior to the start of class, tape up or place colored items around the classroom. Sit in a circle. Teach the children the various color signs as well as the signs for color, I and see. Have the teacher start by signing an example such as: I - see - color - blue. The children have to raise their hands to tell you what they think you spied. Select someone to go to what they think the spied item is and touch it or point. If they select anything with the correct color they win. If they selected the right color but not the right item you continue and see if anyone else can figure it out. After the children have played this a few times then they can be the leader if they guess correctly.

This can also be done with shapes, colors, or both together.

Teach children signs for shapes, color, objects in room.

Jack and the Beanstalk
Children mimic the movements of the character Jack in the story. Can play rhythmic or drum music in the background.
      Jack (children) plants the magic beans on the ground.
          The beans then grow big plants all the way to the sky.
      They climb up the beanstalk into the clouds.
      They begin to walk on the clouds (tip-toe).
      They knock on the door of the castle.
          Nobody answers so they cautiously enter.
      They tip-toe through the castle to avoid the Giant.
      They grab the goose that lays the golden eggs and run back to the beanstalk as fast
          as they can.
      They climb down the beanstalk and get an ax and chop it down.

Teach children signs for plant, magic, ground/dirt, sky, grow, big, climb, clouds, goose/duck, gold, egg.

Ice Skating
Have the children pretend they are figure skaters. Have them take off their shoes and be wearing socks.
      Have them skate in a circle
      Then twirl in place
      Then lift one leg, arms out
      Then lift the other
      Then they skate back to where they normally sit.

Teach children signs for ice skate, circle.

Jumping Beans
Have the children pretend they are jumping beans. First they jump this way, then they jump the other, then they jump repeatedly, then they sit still, then they jump again, until they are all out of jumps.

Teach children signs for jump, sit still.

Jumping Warm Up
Stand in a circle. Show them a jack-in-the-box and how it works. Teach them various signs for different animals they can pretend to be in the box (farm, zoo, ocean, insects). Let them know what animals they are using the animals signs. Have them pop out of the box for each animal making the animal's sounds.

Teach children signs for various animals in the box.

Leonardo's Warm Up
Have the children pretend they are great artists.
    First they build a frame, hammer
    Then they mix their paints, shake
    Then they brush on their paints, paint sign
    Then they dry their painting, wind sign
    Then they clean themselves up, clean sign

Teach children signs for artist, paint, wind, clean up.

Letter Warm Up (Mail)
Stand in a circle. Teach the children various Post Office signs (letter, box, post box, post office, write, stamp). Have them mimic the following actions:
    Letter
    Write the letter
    Fold the letter
    Seal the letter
    Put the letter in the mail box

    Package
    Put the item in the box
    Seal the box with tape
    Address the box
    Carry the box to the car
    Drive the car to the post office
    Carry the package inside and give it to the counter person
    Pay the counter person to send the package

Teach children signs for letter, box, car, post office, mail box.

Meal Time
Sit in a circle. Teach the children the different signs for each meal. Ask if their favorite meal is breakfast, lunch or dinner. One at a time, have them do the sign for the meal that is their favorite.

Teach children signs for breakfast, lunch, snack, dinner.

Meet & Greet
Sit or stand in a circle. Teach the greetings signs to the children (hello, goodbye, how are you today?, okay, fine, wonderful/terrific). Have each child take turns with the teacher saying:
    (child)   Hello, how are you today?
    (teacher)   Okay (fine, wonderful).

    (child)   Goodbye.
    (teacher)   Goodbye.

Let them know that they can now use their sign language to say hello and goodbye every tome they come to class.

Teach children signs for hello, goodbye, fine, okay, wonderful/terrific, how are you today?

Melt Down
Pretend. The snow has fallen. Children begin the process of making a snowman. They roll up the snow into balls and place them on top of one another. Then the sun comes out. Have the children now become the snowman they nave made. As it gets warmer have the children pretend to melt. Down, down, all the way to the ground.

Teach children signs for snow person, balls, sun, warm, down, ground/dirt.

Mighty Wind
Pretend. A storm is coming! A really big one! Everybody under the table!
> Oh, here come the winds (move as if being blown by the wind)
> Now here comes the rain (cover up so as not to get hit by rain)
> Hold on its starting to blow us away (spin around as if being lifted off the ground)
> The storm is over (sit calmly on the floor)

Teach children signs for wind, rain, over/finished.

My Bare Feet
Have the children take off their shoes and socks. Sit in a circle.
> Have the children wiggle their toes
> Then turn their feet in and out as they have their legs on the ground
> Have them bring their legs up and down (repeatedly)
> Have them stomp their feet

Now stand up
> Have the children walk in place
> Then run in place
> Then march in a circle
> Then skip
> Now have them walk on their tip toes in a circle, quiet feet
> Have them slap their feet on the ground, noisy feet
> Then stop and jump up and down (repeatedly)
> Now stop and sit

Teach children signs for shoes, socks, up, down, stomp, run, march, circle, skip, jump, stop, sit.

My Bubble
Have the children use their sign language and also move the movements of the bubble to the song. To the tune of "My Bonnie Lies Over the Ocean".
> My bubble blew over my shoulder (turn around)
> My bubble blew over a tree
> My bubble blew over the playground
> Please blow back my bubble to me, to me
> Blow back, blow back
> Blow back my bubble to me

Teach children signs for bubble, shoulder, tree, over, playground, me.

My Day in the Park
Imagination play activity. Have the children mimic your actions as you go for a day in the park. Leader points out various park attributes in sign such as grass and trees along the way. Add colors to your park and playground signs.
> First you travel to the park in car, drive sign
> Then you get out of the car, open and close the door
> Then you open the gate, go in, and close the gate to the playground (taking turns)
> Then we all go on the swings
> Then we are off to the see-saw
> Then to the climb and slide playground
> After they have played on all of these they chose their favorite to play on
> Then they have to get ready to go by opening, going out, and closing the gate
> Then they walk back to the car and getting in
> Then they drive back home

Teach children signs for playground signs, park signs, colors, drive/car.

My Emotions
Sit in a circle. Teach them the signs for the following emotions: afraid/scared, angry/mad, excited, happy, and love. Have the children respond with the appropriate sign to each of the following statements:
> There was a terrible lightning/thunder storm outside. (afraid/scared)
> The new boy took my favorite toy out of my hand. (angry/mad)
> Mommy (daddy) said we are going to the zoo today. (excited)
> My friend is coming to my house to play. (happy)
> Mommy (daddy) gives me hugs and kisses. (love)

Teach children signs for emotions.

My Favorite
Sit in a circle. Have each of the children tell you the name of their favorite item or thing (animal, food, fruit, vegetable, shape, color, etc.). Help them to form the sign for the item or thing. You can bring in props for each of the topical areas to help.

Teach children signs for animals, foods, fruits, vegetables, shapes, colors, etc.

Name Game
Circle call game. Start with the leader signing her first initial of her name, then that of one of the children, then that child will sign the letter of another child. The game continues until everyone has gone 3 rounds, or more. Help the kids and steer them to make sure everyone is repeatedly called.

Teach children signs for letter of the alphabet.

Pattern Formation
With either rhythmic music in the background or the leader using a drum (4-beat music) have the children follow the stated patterns after they have been demonstrated:
> Push, pull, push, pull
> Up, down, up, down
> Step, hop, step, hop (hop on one leg)
> Step, step, step, hop
> Jump, squat, jump, squat (jump with both legs into the air)
> Slide left, slide right, hop, hop
> Kick right, hop, kick left, hop
> Hop, hop, hop, step
> Push, twist, push, push

Teach children signs for jump, walk, up, down, kick.

Reindeer Romp
To the tune of the "Hokey Pokey"
> You put your antlers in
> You put your antlers out
> You put your antlers in
> And you shake them all about
> You do the Reindeer Romp
> And you turn yourself around
> That's what it's all about

Teach children signs for reindeer, around, antlers.

Ride the Rails
Take several boxes, depending upon the size, and cut the tops and bottoms off. Tape on paper plates for the wheels, you can buy colored or color yourself. On your wall (s), tape posters or pictures of various places to visit in your train. Get ready to roll:
>All aboard, help the children into the boxes and you're off.
>Have the children shuffle their feet together in unison to move the boxes. Visit each of the posted places on the wall(s) and talk about the different sites you may see their. (Cover: nature signs, animal signs, color signs, etc.)
>Talk about the thinks you may see along the way in between sites. (Cover: nature signs, animal signs, etc.)
>After some visits you stop to eat. (Cover: food and meal sings.)

Teach children signs for train, nature, animals, foods, colors.

Roly Poly Races
Set up a start and finish line (cones, tape). Split the team into two teams using your sign language. The car wheels and the truck wheels (can also use bicycle, motorcycle, school bus, tractor, etc.). Line them up and lay them down on their backs to start. Have individual races to the finish line. If they are enjoying this activity then you can use it as a relay race as well.

Teach children signs for the different vehicles that have wheels.

Sounds of Rainbows (Poem)
>*Did you ever hear a rainbow*
>>*With its reds and yellows and blues?*
>*Listen, after a rainstorm,*
>>*While the sun dries off your shoes.*

Teach children signs for rainbow, rain, sun, your, shoes, colors.

Scarecrow
Have children pantomime the following story lines. Sign words to be taught include: child, boy, girl, mother, no, runs, lost, woods, scare-bird (scarecrow), walk.
Part 1 - A child wants to go to the fair, but his/her mother says no. He/she runs away and gets lost in the woods. Where he/she proceeds to fall asleep. As he/she is sleeping she is turned into a scarecrow by a bad woman. Have one of the children get to play the role of the scarecrow.
Part 2 - Many people pass the scarecrow in the woods and are surprised to see it there. Each react differently as they walk by. Have everyone take a turn walking by the scarecrow and help them to express themselves differently.
Part 3 - Have the children create an end to the story and tell you how they would like the boy/girl to be changed back into a person. Then act it out.

Teach children signs for child, boy, girl, mother, no, runs, lost, woods, scare-bird (scarecrow), walk.

Scarf Starter
Stand in a circle. Pass out a scarf to each of the children. Ask them what they can do with a scarf? As they answer, have everybody mimic the stated movement. Toss it up in the air, hide underneath it, wear it, etc.

Teach children signs for scarf, actions.

Shapes
Cut out different shapes (square, circle, triangle, star) in different sizes and colors. Sit in a circle. Have the children tell you using their sign language if they are big or little, as well as what color they are. Then have the children go to different spots on the floor that you have taped various colored shapes on the ground.
     Have all the children go to the red square
     Now go to the yellow star
     Now go to the blue circle
     Now go to the green triangle
     Etc.

Teach children signs for colors, shapes, sizes.

Smelling
Sit in a circle. Pass around various food items that have distinct odors. Such as a lemon, orange, cheese, apple, onion, etc. Teach the sign for each item as it is passed around. Talk about whether it smells sweat or sour? You can also talk about the surface texture, is it smooth or rough? What color are they?

Teach children signs for colors, textures, smells, food signs.

Smoke Crawl
Sit in a circle. Teach the children the sign for fire. Tell them they are going to practice what to do in an emergency, when there is a lot smoke from a fire. Explain that it is very difficult to breath smoke and that it can make you sick or worse. Tell that smoke rises and that it is best to be down low where the air is better. Have them practice by crawling on all fours across the room. Talk about who they should call if there is an emergency, 9-1-1.

Teach children signs for fire, emergency, 9-1-1.

Snow Ball Starter
Imagination play activity. Have the children pretend they are rolling up a really big snowball to make a snowman. Then they have to roll up a second and a third ball and place them on top of the others.

Teach children signs for snow, ball, snow person, roll, big.

Soccer
Stand in a circle. Emphasize taking turns and not cutting in front of others. Make sure all the children can sign the first letter of each others name. As the leader you gently kick the Nerf soccer ball to each one of the children and have them kick it back. Sign the first letter of the name of the person you are kicking the ball to (as well as say it) so they know it is their turn. After everyone has had a turn, have the children gently kick the ball to one another, again signing the name of the person they are going to kick the ball to. Be sure everyone is included in these next rounds.

Teach children signs for soccer, kick, ball, pass, letter of the alphabet.

Storm Winds
Imagination play activity. Set the activity up by telling the children there is a bad storm coming. To need to move together to the safest part of the room together. Once there have them pretend the following actions are happening:
> The wind is blowing really hard
> They are getting very wet from the rain
> The lightning scares everyone
> They have to sit together in their safe place holding hands until the storm passes
> (just a few seconds of quiet to lead into your next activity)

Teach children signs for wind, rain, lightning, scared, everyone, sit, together, storm, passes/finished.

Swimming (strokes in air, swim on floor)
Stand in a circle. Have the children mimic your swim strokes.
> Have the children take long far reaching strokes in the air
> Then have them do the butterfly
> Then have them doggie paddle
Have the children lie on the floor
> Now long strokes with their feet kicking
> Then the backstroke
> Then floating on their back (nice and restful, they have to relax to stay afloat, just a few seconds of quiet to lead into your next activity)

Teach children signs for swim, butterfly, doggie paddle (dog swim).

Tall or Short?
Have the children mimic your movements as you describe different objects as being small, then tall:
> Flower, short, then tall
> Dog, short, then tall
> Tree, short, then tall
> Glass of milk, short, then tall
> Etc.

Teach children signs for flower, short, tall, dog, tree, glass, milk, etc.

Toddler Train
Stand in a circle. Have each of the children turn sideways (the same direction) and grab the shoulders of the person in front of them. Give them each a color. Make a break in your train then head out for your ride in the countryside. Have them make the appropriate "choo choo" sounds as they travel. Talk to them about all the imaginary sites you can see.

First we see a farm, with cows, horses, pigs, chickens, dogs, cats, ducks, etc.
Then we come to the park where we see boys and girls playing.
Etc.

Teach children signs for train, colors, farm animals, boys, girls, playing.

Toy Store
Sit in a circle. Have the children decide what toy they want to be. Teach the sign for toy and the first letter of each of the different toys the children have selected. They could be a train, truck, plane, doll, superhero, etc. Then place them in character positions around the room, in the freeze position.
Part 1 - The leader is the storekeeper who goes around the room and adjusts the toys and dusts them off. A child selected to be the customer comes in and the storekeeper shows her the toys one at a time. Each toy demonstrates what they can do as it is being shown off. The 1st customer does not by any toys.
Part 2 - That evening after the store closes and the storekeeper goes home the toys come alive and play with one another. They want to stay together and so they make a plan to pretend they are broken so they will not be sold.
Part 3 - The storekeeper returns in the morning. She decides to have a toy "SALE". So she makes up a sign and puts it in the window. Once again all the toys have to freeze in place.
Part 4 - A 2nd customer comes into the store. The storekeeper shows them around, but strangely enough all the toys now move as if they were broken.
Part 5 - The storekeeper takes all the "broken" toys to the local church preschool to donate them to the church. The toys are so happy that they will get to stay together and that they now will all have boys and girls to play with. Storekeeper takes the toys to the church, where they immediately begin playing with all the children and each other.

Teach children signs for toy, letters of the alphabet, child, boys, girls, play.

Travel Starter
Sit in a circle. Explain to the children that they are going on a make believe trip together. Tell them that they will be using many different types of vehicles along the way. They need to mimic the movements for each. Noises to accompany the signs are recommended.

First they are traveling in a truck to the airport
Then they are flying in an airplane to the shore
Then they are driving in a car to the ocean
Then they are going on a sail boat to a beautiful island
Then they are going for a walk on the sandy beach
After a couple of days of fun on the island they head for home

Teach children signs for truck, airplane, car, ocean, beautiful, beach, walk, fun, home.

Under the Sea
Sit in a circle. Talk about what it would be like to be under the sea and the various sea and ocean animal signs. Discuss how the animals and plants move in the water and their colors. Pictures from magazines or books are great to show them. A water moving relaxation CD could be used as background music.
Part 1 - Have the children move as if they were swimming underwater. Remind them that water is heavier than air so they need to move their arms and legs slowly.
Part 2 - Have the children sway back and forth as if they were plants.
Part 3 - Now have them move as if they were fish. Talk about the difference in the movements of the big fish and the little fish. Have them be small fast moving fish, then have them be large slow moving whales.
Part 4 - Talk about other animals that you may find under the sea, such as a sea turtle or an octopus.

Teach children signs for swim, ocean/sea, plants, ocean animals, fish.

Volleyball
Have the children split into two groups. One on either side of the net (tennis height or streamer). The object is to tap the ball over the net before it hits the ground. Children can hit the ball as many times as they need to get it across. There is no keeping score and multiple balls should be used simultaneously for fun and involvement of all. Have the children rotate from front to back rows if needed to insure participation by everyone. You can use beach balls, balloons or both to play.

Teach children signs for colors of the balls, ball, hit, fun, play.

Vote
Sit in a circle. Have the children vote for their favorite item or thing (animal, food, fruit, vegetable, shape, color, etc.) by signing the name of the item or thing as it is called.

Teach children signs for animal, food, fruit, vegetable, shape, color, etc.

Waddle-a-way
Teach children the sign for duck. Have them mimic the movement of a duck, close down to the ground, as they waddle along and reproduce the sign for duck. Duck sounds are also welcome. Have them waddle around an object of two, or have them go to a certain point and return to the circle.

Teach children signs for duck.

Water, Water Everywhere
Pretend/exercise.
>We are in water up to our knees, wading
>Now we are in up to our belly buttons
>Now we are in up to our shoulders
>Now we are over our heads
>How can we swim?
>>On top of the water
>>Backstroke
>>Float
>>Underwater.
>What do we see?
>Fish, sharks, whales, plants, sand, rocks
>Oh no, someone pulled the plug, bath time is over!

Teach children signs for body parts, swim, water, fish, sharks, whales, plants, sand, rocks.

Wing Warm Up
Stand in a circle. Tape a piece of construction paper to the wrist and forearm of each child. Tell that these are wings. Talk about different things that have wings such as planes or birds. Have them work as a group following your lead:
>As a Bird
>Flap your wings
>Soar - right, then left

>As a Plane
>Taking off - turn wings down
>Turning - right, then left
>Landing - turn wings up

Teach children signs for fly, planes, birds, down, up.

Who Is the Biggest?
Sit in a circle. Using, pictures, stuffed animals or sounds, have the children help you put the animals in order from the smallest to the largest. Act out each of the animal's movements and sounds. Can also be done with zoo or ocean animals.

Teach children signs for big, small, farm animals.

Wonder Shoes
Imagination play activity. Have the children experience what it is like to walk a bit in someone else's shoes. Types of shoes you can try are as follows:

Have the children try on space boots
Then try on cowboy boots
Then ballet slippers
Then snow shoes
Then basketball shoes
Then swim fins
Then clown shoes
Then line them up to try on running shoes

Teach children signs for shoes, snow, basketball, swim, clown/silly, run.

CHAPTER 10:
TOPICAL HANDOUTS

LET'S SIGN AND SING TOGETHER!

Handouts - Index

Animal Alphabet

"The Alphabet Song" - Traditional

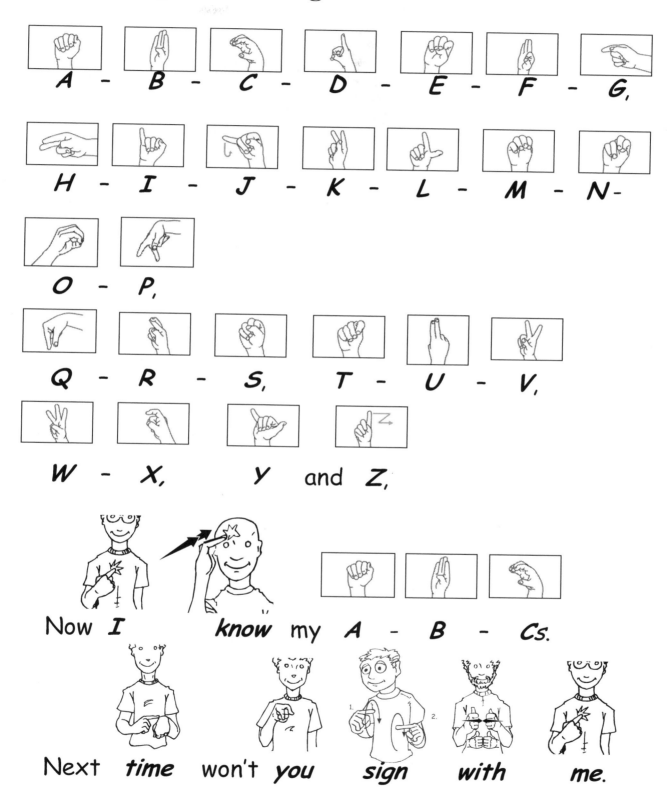

A - B - C - D - E - F - G,

H - I - J - K - L - M - N-

O - P,

Q - R - S, T - U - V,

W - X, Y and Z,

Now *I* know my A - B - Cs.

Next *time* won't *you* sign with me.

Aa

ant

apple

Bb

bumble bee

bear

C c

candy

clown

Dd

dog   duck

Ee

Egg

Elephant

Ff

flower

frog

Gg

garden

goat

Hh

horse

house

Ii

ice cream

iguana

Jj

jaguar

jacket

Kk
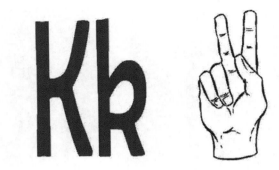

kite

kangaroo

Ll

lemon

lady bug

Mm

muffin

magic

Nn

nut

newt

Oo

octopus

owl

Pp

peach

pig

Qq

queen

quarter

Rr

rabbit

raspberry

Ss

sun

sea turtle

Tt

tiger

train

Uu

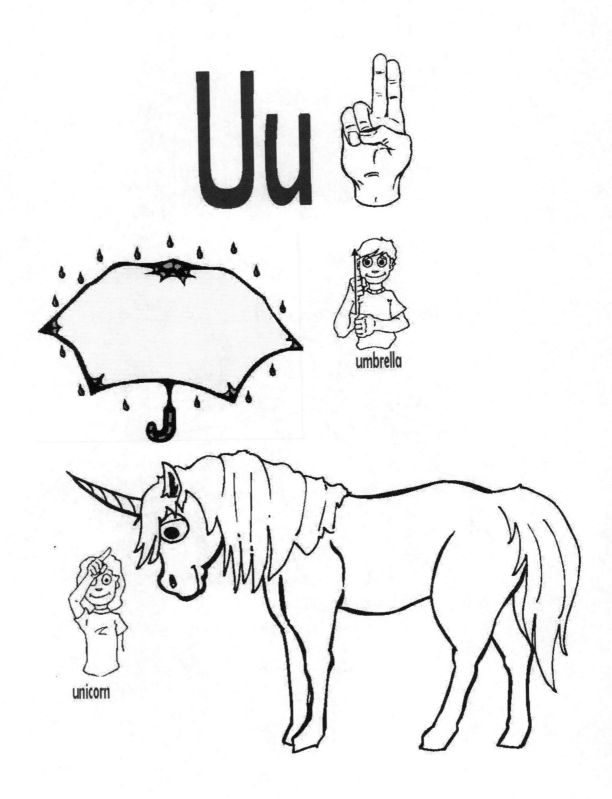

umbrella

unicorn

Vv

vulture

violin

Ww

water

whale

Xx

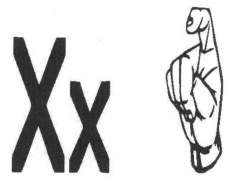

xylophone

x-ray fish

Yy

yo-yo

yack

Zz

zipper

zebra

EMOTIONS

angry-enojado(a)

happy - alegre, feliz

sorry – lo siento

sad - triste

"Three Little Monkeys"
(Traditional)

Three   *little*   *monkeys*   *swinging*   in a   *tree*

Teasing   Mr. *Alligator*   *can't*   *catch*   *me*

Along   *came*   the   *alligator*   as   *quiet*   as   can   be

Snap   that   *monkey*   *off*   the   *tree*

Two   *little*   *monkeys* ......

One   *little*   *monkey* .....

No more   *monkeys*   *swinging*   in a   *tree.*

Animals on the Farm — Copyright Time to Sign, Inc. 2002

(Tune: The Wheels on the Bus)
The cows on the farm say: "Moo, moo, moo; moo, moo, moo; moo, moo, moo"
The cows on the farm say: "Moo, moo, moo"
All around the farm

The ducks on the farm say: "Quack, quack, quack; quack, quack, quack; quack, quack, quack"
The ducks on the farm say: "Quack, quack, quack"
All around the farm

The pigs on the farm say: "Oink, oink, oink; oink, oink, oink; oink, oink, oink
The pigs on the farm say: "Oink, oink, oink"
All around the farm

The sheep on the farm say: " Baa, baa, baa; baa, baa, baa; baa, baa, baa"
The sheep on the farm say: " Baa, baa, baa"
All around the farm

The chickens on the farm say: "Cluck, cluck, cluck; cluck, cluck, cluck; cluck, cluck, cluck"
The chickens on the farm say: "Cluck, cluck, cluck"
All around the farm

The horse on the farm says: "Neigh, neigh, neigh; neigh, neigh, neigh; neigh, neigh, neigh"
The horse on the farm says: "Neigh, neigh, neigh"
All round the farm

The cats on the farm say: "Meow, meow, meow; meow, meow, meow; meow, meow, meow"
The cats on the farm say: "Meow, meow, meow"
All around the farm

The dog on the farm says: "Ruff, ruff, ruff; ruff, ruff, ruff; ruff, ruff, ruff"
The dog on the farm says: "Ruff, ruff, ruff"
All around the farm

The farmer on the farm says: "Come'on and eat, come'on and eat,
Its time to eat"
The farmer on the farm says: "Come'on and eat"
All around the farm

 cow - vaca

 duck - pato

 pig - cerdo

 sheep - oveja

 chicken - pollo

 horse - caballo

 cat - gato

 dog - perro

Old MacDonald Had A Farm - Traditional

Old Macdonald had a farm ee-eye, ee-eye oh
And on that farm he had a duck, ee-eye, ee-eye, oh
With a quack, quack here and a quack, quack there
Here a quack, there a quack, everywhere a quack, quack
Old Macdonald had a farm ee-eye, ee-eye oh

Old Macdonald had a farm, ee-eye, ee-eye oh
And on that farm he had a cow, ee-eye, ee-eye oh
With a moo, moo here, and a moo, moo there
Here a moo, there a moo, everywhere a moo, moo
Quack, quack here, and a quack, quack there
Here a quack, there a quack, everywhere a quack, quack
Old Macdonald had a farm ee-eye, ee-eye oh

Old Macdonald had a farm ee-eye, ee-eye oh
And on that farm he had a dog, ee-eye, ee-eye oh
With a woof, woof here, and a woof, woof there
Here a woof, there a woof, everywhere a woof, woof
Moo, moo here, and a moo, moo there
Here a moo, there a moo, everywhere a moo, moo
Quack, quack here, and a quack, quack there
Here a quack, there a quack, everywhere a quack, quack
Old Macdonald had a farm ee-eye, ee-eye oh

Old Macdonald had a farm ee-eye, ee-eye oh
And on that farm he had a pig, ee-eye, ee-eye oh
With an oink, oink here, and an oink, oink there
Here an oink, there an oink, everywhere an oink, oink
Woof, woof here, and a woof, woof there
Here a woof, there a woof, everywhere a woof, woof
Moo, moo here, and a moo, moo there
Here a moo, there a moo, everywhere a moo, moo
Quack, quack here, and a quack, quack there
Here a quack, there a quack, everywhere a quack, quack
Old Macdonald had a farm ee-eye, ee-eye oh

duck - pato

cow - vaca

dog - perro

pig - cerdo

FAMILY

mother - madre

father - padre

brother - hermano

sister -hermana

family - familia

"Five Little Monkeys"
(Traditional)

Five little monkeys jumping on the *bed*,

One fell off and bumped his *head*.

Mama called the *doctor* and the *doctor said*,

"*No more monkeys jumping* on the *bed*."

Four little monkeys . . .

Three little monkeys . . .

Two little monkeys . . .

One little monkey . . .

monkey - mono

www.timetosign.com

COLORS

black – negro

blue - azul

brown – marron

colors - colores

gold – oro

gray - gris

green - verde

orange - anaranjado

peach – melocotó

COLORS

red - rojo

silver – plata

tan - bronceado

white - blanco

yellow - amarillo

pink - rosa

purple - púrpura

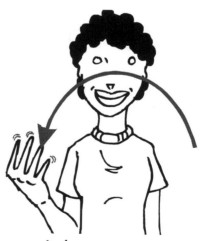

rainbow – arco iris

SHAPES

circle - circulo

diamond - diamante

heart- corazón

oval - ovalado

OCEAN ANIMALS

fish - pez

shark - tiburón

starfish - estrella del mar

whale - ballena

"Clean Up"

(Original Author Unknown, Illustrations Copyright©2004 Time to Sign, Inc.)

Clean up, Clean up   everybody everywhere

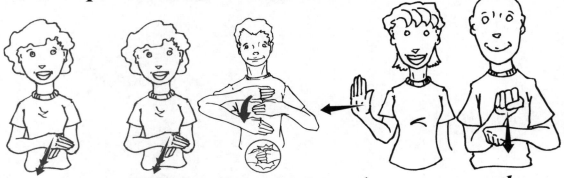

Clean up, Clean up everybody do **your   share**
(work)

"Please and Thank You"
(Original Author Unknown, Illustrations Copyright©2002 Time to Sign, Inc.)

Please   and   *thank you*

Please   and   *thank you*

magic   **words**   *magic*   **words.**

Time to Sign, inc.

Everyone   should   *use*   them.

Everyone   should   *use*   them

Everyday - swipe hand across the cheek 3 times.

Everyday   *everyday.*

"If You're Hungry and You Know It"

(Traditional, Illustrations Copyright©2004 Time to Sign, Inc.)

If *you're*   *hungry*   and you *know* it, clap *your hands.* (clap, clap)
Repeat

If *you're*   *hungry* and you *know* it,   *your*   *face* will surely *show* it.
If *you're hungry* and you *know* it, clap *your hands.* (clap, clap)

If *you're*   *thirsty* and you   *know* it,   *say,* "boo, hoo." (pretend to cry)
Repeat

Time to Sign Inc.

If *you're* *thirsty* and you *know* it,　　*your*　　*face* will surely *show* it.
If *you're thirsty* and you *know* it, say, "boo, hoo." (pretend to cry)

If *you're*　　*hungry* and you *know* it, stomp your feet. (stomp, stomp)
Repeat

If *you're*　　*hungry* and you *know* it,　　*your*　　*face* will surely *show* it.
　If *you're hungry* and you *know* it, stomp your feet. (stomp, stomp)

"Where Are My Pets?"
(Copyright©2002 Time to Sign, Inc.)

Where is *kitty*?　　*Where* is *kitty*?

Here　*I* am.　　*Here*　*I* am.

How are *you*　*today*? Very *sleepy* I say.

Stretch your front paws, stretch your back paws. (make stretching motion)

Where is *puppy*?　　*Where* is *puppy*?

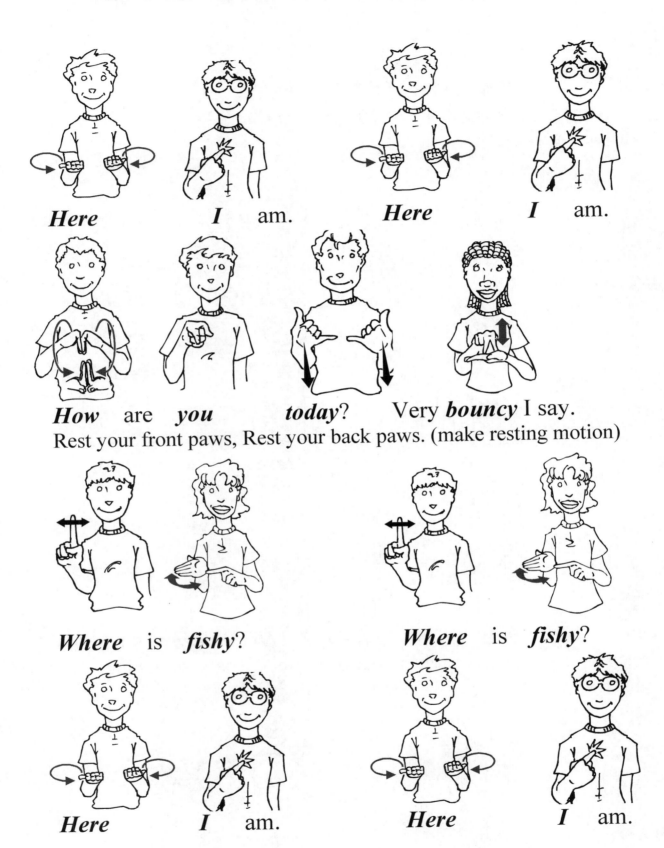

Here   *I*   am.   *Here*   *I*   am.

How   are   *you*   *today*?   Very *bouncy* I say.

Rest your front paws, Rest your back paws. (make resting motion)

Where   is   *fishy*?   *Where*   is   *fishy*?

Here   *I*   am.   *Here*   *I*   am.

How are ***you*** ***today***? Very ***happy*** I say.
Stretch your top fin, stretch your tail fin. (make stretching motion)

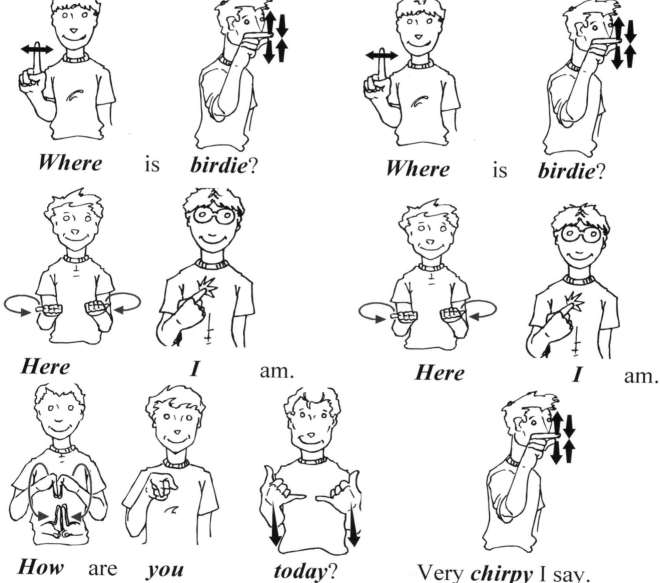

Where is ***birdie***?   ***Where*** is ***birdie***?

Here ***I*** am.   ***Here*** ***I*** am.

How are ***you*** ***today***? Very ***chirpy*** I say.
Flap your one wing, flap your other wing.
(make flapping motions)

Where are **my** **pets**? **Where** are **my** **pets**?

Here **we** are. **Here** **we** are.

How are **you** **today**? Very **lively** we say.

Let's **go** **play**. (Repeat)

"Seven Days"

(Traditional, Illustrations Copyright©2002 Time to Sign, Inc.)

There   are   *seven*   *days*, there   are   *seven*   *days*,

there   are   *seven*   *days*   in   a   *week*.

Sunday,   *Monday,*   *Tuesday,*   *Wednesday,*

Thursday,   *Friday,*   *Saturday.*

"*Twinkle Twinkle Little Star*"
(Traditional, Illustrations Copyright©2004 Time to Sign, Inc.)

Twinkle,   *twinkle*,   *little*   *star*,

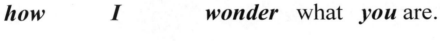

how   *I*   *wonder*   what   *you*   are.

Up   *above*   the   *world*   so   high,

like   a   *diamond*   in   the   *sky*.

Twinkle,   *twinkle*,   *little*   *star*,

how   *I*   *wonder*   what   *you*   are.

"Row, Row, Row Your Boat"

((Traditional, Illustrations Copyright©2002 Time to Sign, Inc.)

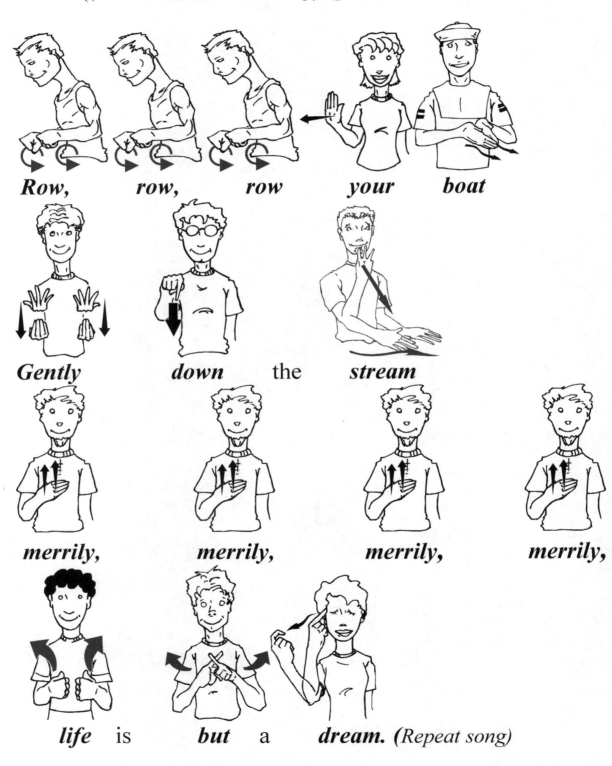

Row,   *row,*   *row*   *your*   *boat*

Gently   *down*   the   *stream*

merrily,   *merrily,*   *merrily,*   *merrily,*

life is *but* a *dream.* *(Repeat song)*

"We've Been Playing"

(Original Author Unknown, Tune of "I've been working on the railroad",
Illustrations Copyright©2002 Time to Sign, Inc.)

We've been *playing* on the *playground*

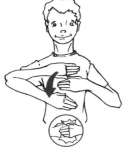 

all the *morning* long.

We've been *playing* in the *playground*

having *fun* and *singing* songs.

Now   it's   *time*   to   *brush the dust off,*

go   in   and   *eat*   our   *lunch.*

Then   *we'll*   *brush our teeth*   and   *lay down,*

look   out   *here*   *we*   *come.*

"I'm a Firefighter"
(Original Author Unknown, Tune of "I'm a Little Teapot, Illustrations Copyright©2003 Time to Sign, Inc.)

I'm   a   *firefighter*

dressed   in *red,*

with   *my*   *fire hat*

on   *my*   *head.*

I can **drive** the **fire** **truck,**

fight **fires,** **too,**

and **help** to **make** things

safe for **you.**

"I'm a Police Officer"

(Original Author Unknown, Tune of "I'm a Little Teapot, Illustrations Copyright©2003 Time to Sign, Inc.)

I'm a   *police officer*

with   *my*   *star,*

I   *help*   *people*

near and   *far.*

If *you* have a *problem*,

call   on   *me*,

and *I* will be *there*

one,   *two,*   *three!*

"I'm a Little Letter"

(Original Author Unknown, tune of "I'm a Little Teapot", Illustrations
Copyright©2004 Time to Sign, Inc.)

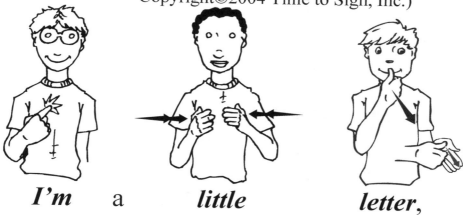

I'm   a   *little*   *letter*,

nice   and   *fat*.

Here is *my* *address*,

TimetoSign inc.

and *here* is *my* **stamp**.

Drop *me* in a **mailbox**

then *watch* *me* *go*

Sending *my* *love* **around** the **world**.

"My Dentist"

(Original Author Unknown, tune of "Are You Sleeping?", Illustrations
Copyright©2004 Time to Sign, Inc.)

My *Dentist* *tells me,*

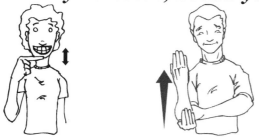

Brush your teeth, Brush your teeth.

Brush them in the *morning*

and *again* at *bedtime*.

"London Bridge"

(Traditional, Illustrations Copyright©2003 Time to Sign, Inc.)

London   *bridge*   is   *falling down, falling down, falling down.*

London   *bridge*   is   *falling down*

my   *fair*   *lady.*

Build   it up *with*   *iron*   *bars,*

Time to Sign inc.

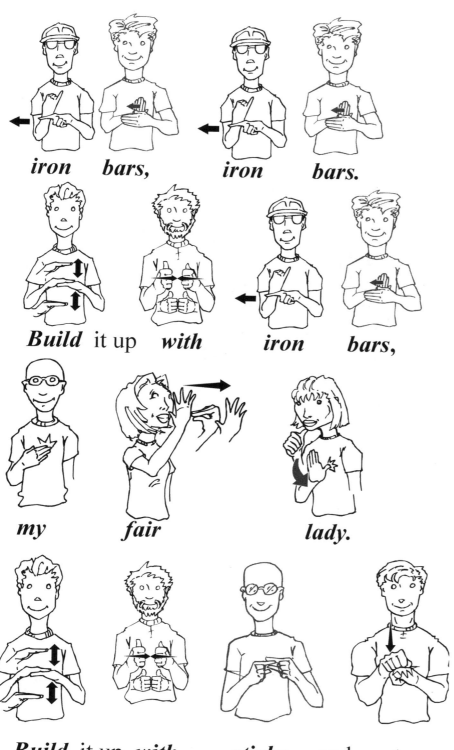

iron   bars,   iron   bars.

Build it up **with** iron bars,

my   fair   lady.

Build it up **with** sticks and stones

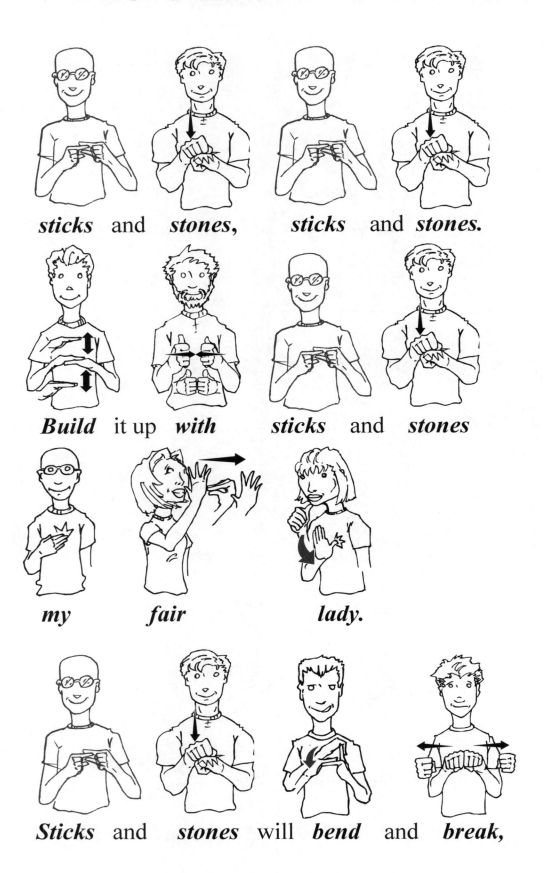

sticks   and   *stones,*   *sticks*   and   *stones.*

Build   it up   *with*   *sticks*   and   *stones*

my   *fair*   *lady.*

Sticks   and   *stones*   will   *bend*   and   *break,*

bend and *break,* *bend* and *break.*

Sticks and *stones* will *bend* and *break*

my *fair* *lady.*

"Car Song"

(Original Author Unknown, Illustrations Copyright©2002 Time to Sign, Inc.)

We   *like*   to   *travel*   *in*   our   *car*
Hurrah, Hurrah.

A *car*   *can*   *take*   *us*   *near*   or   *far*
Hurrah, Hurrah.

We   *buckle*   up   *before*   *we*   *go,*

Time to Sign inc.

whether   *we're*   *going*   *fast*   or   *slow.*

So *we'll*   *all*   be   *safer* while *riding* in   *our*   *car*
Beep, beep, beep, beep
Beep, beep, beep, beep.

"Wheels on the Bus"
(Traditional, Illustrations Copyright©2002-2003 Time to Sign, Inc.)

The ***wheels*** ***on*** the ***bus*** go ***round*** and ***round,***

round and ***round,*** ***round*** and ***round***
The wheels on the bus go round and round, (repeat)

all ***through*** the ***town.***

The ***wipers on*** the ***bus*** go ***swish, swish, swish,***

swish, swish, swish,   ***swish, swish, swish***

The wipers on the bus go swish, swish, swish, (repeat)

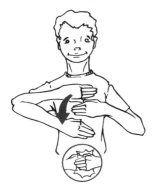  

all   ***through*** the ***town.***

The ***horn on*** the ***bus*** goes ***beep, beep, beep,***

beep, *beep*, *beep*,   *beep*, *beep*, *beep*

The horn on the bus goes beep, beep, beep, (repeat)

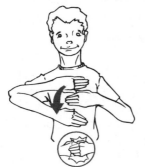  

all   *through*   the   *town.*

The *baby*   *on*   the   *bus*   goes   *waa, waa, waa,*

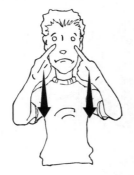 

waa, *waa*, *waa*,   *waa, waa, waa,*

The baby on the bus goes waa, waa, waa, (repeat)

all *through* the *town.*

The *mommy* *on* the *bus* goes *shh, shh, shh,*

shh, shh, shh, *shh, shh, shh*

The mommy on the bus goes shh, shh, shh, (repeat)

all *through* the *town.*

The *driver* *on* the *bus* goes *move* on *back,*

move on *back,* *move* on *back*

The driver on the bus goes move on back, (repeat)

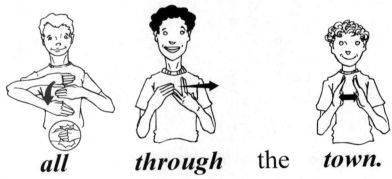

all *through* the *town.*

The *wheels* *on* the *bus* go *round* and *round,*

round and ***round,***   ***round*** and ***round***

The wheels on the bus go round and round, (repeat)

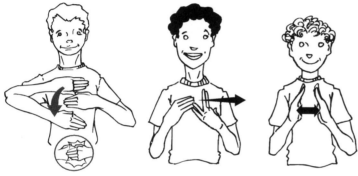

all   ***through*** the ***town.***

"Little Red Caboose"

(Original Author Unknown, Illustrations Copyright©2004 Time to Sign, Inc.)

Little   **red**   **caboose,**
Little   **red**   **caboose,**

Little   **red**   **caboose behind** the **train, train**

Smoke-stack on his   **back,**   **going** down the **track,**

Little   **red**   **caboose behind** the **train, train**

"Buckle Bear Safety Song"
(Original Author Unknown, Illustrations Copyright©2003 Time to Sign, Inc.)

I   *like*   **my**   *seatbelt*

nice   and   **snug**

around   my   **hips**

like   a   **big**   **bear**   **hug.**

I *make* it *click*

so the *driver* will *know*

I'm *buckled* up and *ready* to *go.*

"Down by the Bay"

(Traditional, Illustrations Copyright©2004 Time to Sign, Inc.)

Down by the **bay**, where the **watermelons** grow

Back to my **home** **I** **dare** not **go**, (shake head)

For if **I** **do** **my** **mother** will **say**,

Did **you** ever **see** a **bear** **combing** his **hair**?

Down by the **bay**

Additional Verses

...**llamas**   **eating**   **their**   **pajamas,**

... a **goat**   **standing**   in a **boat**?

... a *cat* wearing a *hat?*

...a *lion* when he was *crying?*

...a *shark playing* in the *park?*

"*Bear Went Over the Mountain, The*"
(Traditional, Illustrations Copyright©2003 Time to Sign, Inc.)

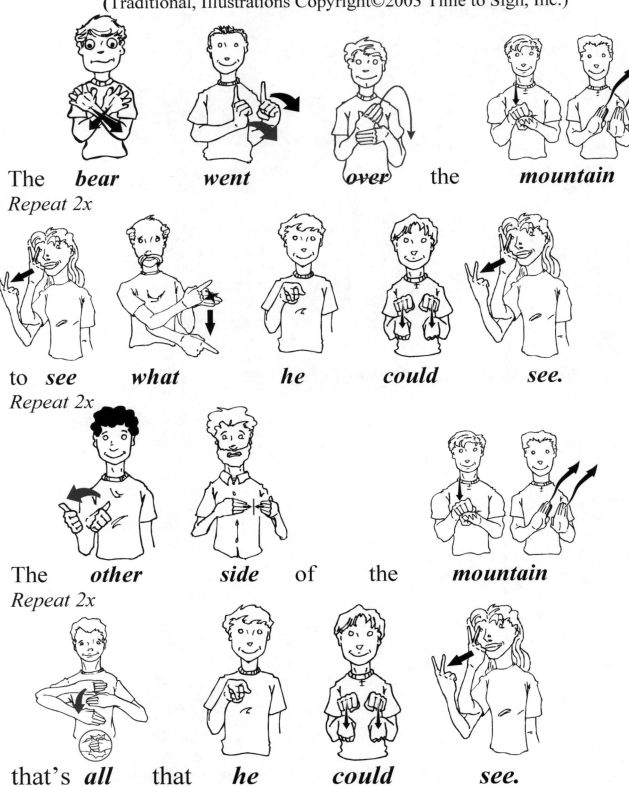

The   ***bear***   ***went***   ***over***   the   ***mountain***
Repeat 2x

to   ***see***   ***what***   ***he***   ***could***   ***see.***
Repeat 2x

The   ***other***   ***side***   of   the   ***mountain***
Repeat 2x

that's   ***all***   that   ***he***   ***could***   ***see.***

"Mr. Sun"

(Traditional, Illustrations Copyright©2002 Time to Sign, Inc.)

Oh Mister *Sun*, *sun*, Mister *Golden* *Sun*

please *shine* down *on* *me.*

Oh Mister *Sun*, *sun*, Mister *Golden* *Sun*

hiding *behind* a *tree*.

These *little*   *children*   are *asking*   *you*

to   *please*   *come*   *out*

so   *we*   *can*   *play*   *with*   *you.*

Oh Mister *Sun,*   *sun,*   Mister *Golden*   *Sun*

please　　*shine*　　down,

please　　*shine*　　down,

please　　*shine*　　down　　*on*　　*me.*

"Bumble Bee"
(Traditional, Illustrations Copyright©2002 Time to Sign, Inc.)

I'm　*bringin'*　*home*　a　*baby*　*bumble bee*

won't　*my*　*mommy*　be so　*proud*　of　*me.*
(chorus)

I'm　*bringin'*　*home*　a　*baby*　*bumble bee*

ouch,　it　*stung*　*me*! (chorus)

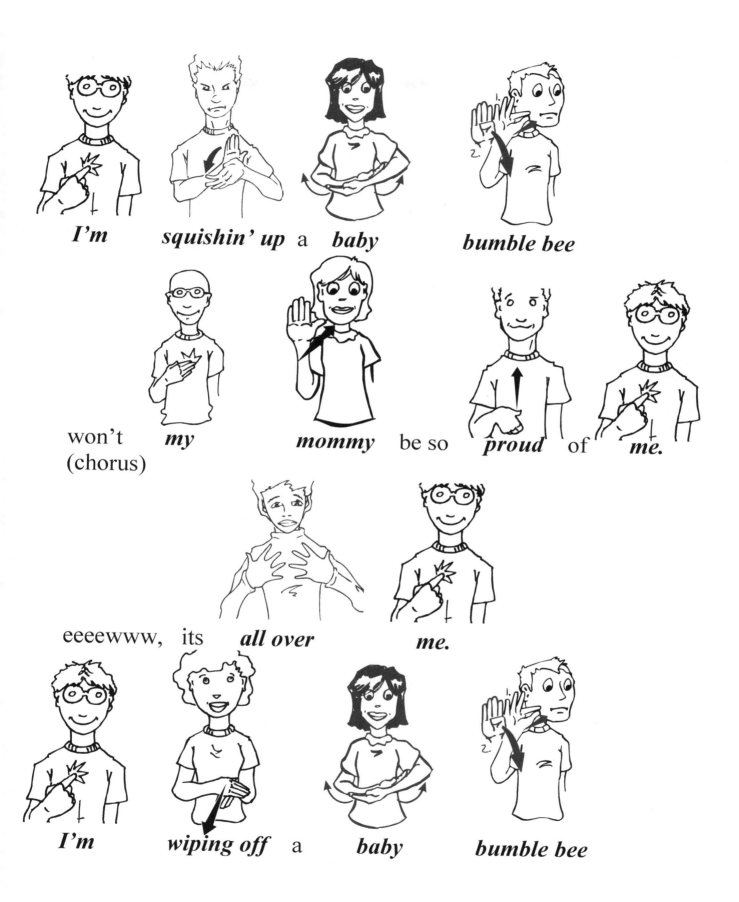

I'm   *squishin' up* a   *baby*   *bumble bee*

won't   *my*   *mommy*   be so   *proud*   of   *me.*
(chorus)

eeeewww,   its   *all over*   *me.*

I'm   *wiping off* a   *baby*   *bumble bee*

won't   *my*   *mommy*   be so   *proud*   of   *me.*

I'm   *wiping off*   a   *baby*   *bumble bee*

won't   *my*   *mommy*   be so   *proud*   of   *me.*

There,   *all clean*!

"Itsy Bitsy Spider"
(Traditional, Illustrations Copyright©2002 Time to Sign, Inc.)

The *itsy, bitsy* spider went up the *water spout*.

Down came the *rain,* and *washed* the *spider* *out*.

Up came the *sun* and *dried* up all the *rain*.

And the *itsy, bitsy spider* went *up* the spout *again*.
Repeat song

"Rain, Rain Go Away"

(Original Author Unknown, Illustrations Copyright©2004 Time to Sign, Inc.)

Rain, rain   **go away**

Come again some **other**   **day**

We   want   to go   outside and **play**

Come again some **other**   **day.**

"You Are My Sunshine"

(Traditional, Illustrations Copyright©2003 Time to Sign, Inc.)

You   are   *my*   *sunshine,*

one   of   *my*   *sunshine's.*

You *make* *me* *happy,* *when* *skies* are *gray.*

Time to Sign inc.

You'll   *always*   *know*   dear,

how much   *I*   *love*   *you.*

Please   *don't*   *take*   *my*   *sunshine*   *away.*

"Over the River and Through the Woods"
(Traditional, Illustrations Copyright©2003 Time to Sign, Inc.)

Over the *river* and *through* the *woods*

to *grandmother's* *house* *we* *go.*

The *horse* *knows* the *way* to

carry the *sleigh* *through* *white*

Time to Sign inc.

and drifting *snow.*

Over   the   *river*   and   *through*   the   *woods*

oh   how   the   *wind*   does   *blow*!

(Point to toes)

It   *stings*   the   **toes**   and   *bites*   the   **nose**

As   *over*   the   *fields*   *we*   *go.*

"It's Summer Time Again"

(Copyright©2003 Time to Sign, Inc., Tune of "The Farmer in the Dell")

It's **Summer** *time* **again**, *(Repeat 1x)*

what   a   *time*   *we*   will   *have*

it's **Summer**   *time*   **again**.

 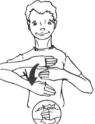  

We'll   **all**   **go**   to the   **beach**, *(Repeat 1x)*

Time to Sign Inc.

what   a   *time*   *we*   will   *have*

we'll   *all*   *go*   to the   *beach*.

We'll   *all*   *go*   out and   *camp,* *(Repeat 1x)*

what   a   *time*   *we*   will   *have*

We'll   *all*   *go* out and *camp.*

We'll   *all*   *go*   *picnicking,* (Repeat 1x)

what a *time*   *we*   will   *have*

We'll   *all*   *go*   *picnicking.*

We'll *watch* the *baseball* *game* (Repeat 1x)

what a *time* *we* will *have*

we'll *watch* the *baseball* *game.*

We'll *see* the *fireworks* *(Repeat 1x)*

what a **time** **we** will **have** *(Repeat 2x)*

We'll **see** the **fireworks.**

"I'm a Little Bubble"

(Original Author Unknown, tune of "I'm a Little Teapot", Illustrations
Copyright©2004 Time to Sign, Inc.)

I'm   a   ***little***   ***bubble,***

Shiny   and   ***round.***

I gently float ***down*** to the ***ground.***

The ***wind***   ***lifts*** me up and then I ***drop.***

Down to the ***dry ground*** where I ***pop.***

"Shirts, Pants, Shoes, and Socks"

(Copyright©2004 Time to Sign, Inc., Tune of "Head, Shoulders, Knees, and Toes")

Shirt, **pants,** **shoes** and **socks.**

Shoes and **socks.**

(Repeat)

Dress, and **skirt,** and **hat,** and **coat.**

Shirt, pants, **shoes** and **socks.**

Shoes **and** **socks.**

"I'm a Little Teapot"

(Traditional, Illustrations Copyright©2004 Time to Sign, Inc.)

I'm a *little* *teapot* *short* and *stout*

Here is my handle, here is my spout

When *I* get all *steamed up*,

hear *me* *shout*

Just tip me over and *pour* me out.

"I'm a Little Flower"

(Original Author Unknown, tune of "I'm a Little Teapot", Illustrations
Copyright©2004 Time to Sign, Inc.)

I'm   a   *little*   *flower*   *green* and *red*

I   grew up   in a *flower   bed*

With a *little*   *rain*   and tender *care*

Flowers, flowers, everywhere.

"March and Sing"

(Original Author Unknown, tune of "The Mulberry Bush", Illustrations
Copyright©2004 Time to Sign, Inc.)

Along the *trail*   *we march* and *sing,*

March and *sing,*   *march* and *sing.*

Along the *trail*   *we*   *march* and *sing,*

along the *trail*   *today.*

Additional Verses: We huff and puff (breathe heavily); swing our arms (swing arms back and forth at sides)

SPORTS - I

baseball –
béisbol

basketball –
baloncesto

football –
fútbol

hockey –
hockey

soccer -
balonpie

volleyball -
vóleibol

SPORTS - II

ball - bola

throw – tirar

catch – coger

golf – golf

swimming – nadar

ice skating – pantinar sobre hielo

"Colors, Colors Everywhere"

(Original Author Unknown, Tune of "I've Been Working on the Railroad",
Illustrations Copyright©2004 Time to Sign, Inc.)

Red is the *color* for an *apple* to *eat.*

Red is the *color* for *cherries*, too.

Red is the *color* for *strawberries*,

I   *like*   *red*, don't *you*?

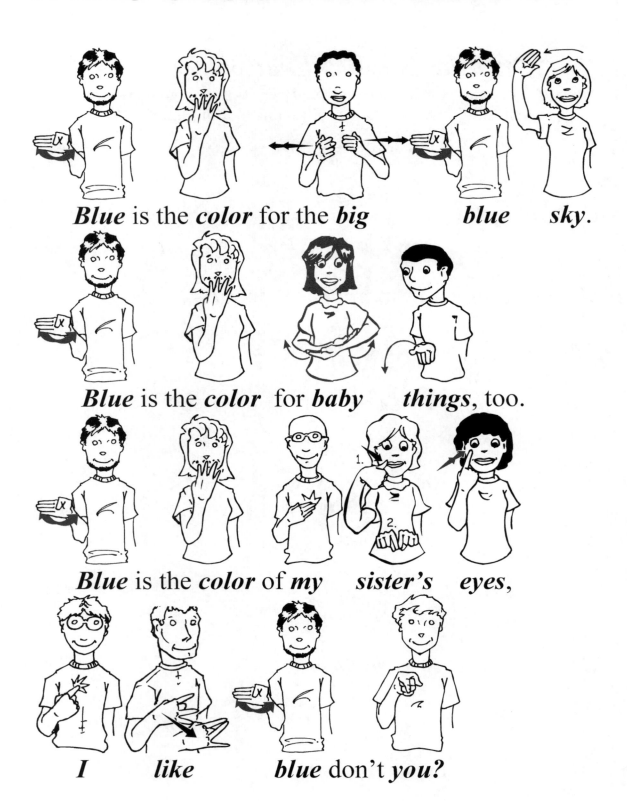

Blue is the *color* for the *big* *blue* *sky*.

Blue is the *color* for *baby* *things*, too.

Blue is the *color* of *my* *sister's* *eyes*,

I *like* *blue* don't *you?*

Time to Sign inc.

Yellow is the *color* for the great *big*   *sun*.

Yellow is the *color* for   *lemonade*, too.

Yellow is the *color* of a *baby*   *chick*,

I   *like*   *yellow* don't *you*

Green is the *color* for the *leaves*   *on* the *trees*.

Green is the *color* for *green*   *peas*, too.

Green is the *color* for a *watermelon*,

I   *like*   *green*, don't *you?*

Orange is the *color* for *oranges*.

Orange is the *color* for *carrots*, too.

Orange is the *color* of a *jack-o'-lantern*,

I   *like*   *orange*, don't *you?*

Purple is the *color* for a bunch of *grapes*.

Purple is the *color* for *grape* *juice*, too.

Purple is the *color* for a *violet*,

I *like* *purple*, don't *you?*

"Head, Shoulders, Knees, and Toes"
(Traditional, Illustrations Copyright©2004 Time to Sign, Inc.)

(Touch Shoulders)

Head,   **Shoulders,**   **Knees**

(Point to Toes)

and **Toes**

(Point to Toes)

Knees   and   **Toes**

(Repeat)

(Point to Mouth)

Eyes, and   **Ears,**   and   **Mouth,** and **Nose**

(Touch Shoulders)   *(Point to Toes)*

Head,   **Shoulders,**   **Knees** and **Toes**

(Point to Toes)

Knees   and   **Toes**

MONTHS - I

January –
Enero

February –
Febrero

March –
Marzo

April –
Abril

May –
Mayo

June –
Junio

MONTHS - II

July –
Julio

August –
Agosto

September –
Septiembre

October –
Octubre

November –
Noviembre

December –
Diciembre

"Jingle Bells"

(Traditional, Illustrations Copyright©2004 Time to Sign, Inc.)

Dashing through the **snow**   in a **one-horse** open **sleigh**

O'er the   **fields**   **we**   **go**

Laughing   **all**   the   **way**

Bells on bobtail **ring** **making** spirits **bright**

Time to Sign inc.

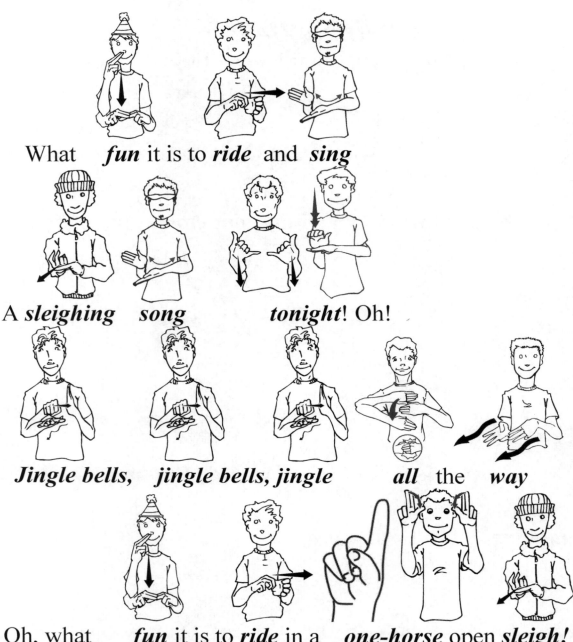

What   *fun* it is to *ride* and *sing*

A *sleighing*   *song*   *tonight*! Oh!

Jingle bells,   *jingle bells, jingle*   *all*   the   *way*

Oh, what   *fun* it is to *ride* in a   *one-horse* open *sleigh!*
Hey!
(Repeat)

"We Wish You A Merry Christmas"
(Traditional, Illustrations Copyright©2004 Time to Sign, Inc.)

We   *wish*   *you*   a   *merry* **Christmas** *(Repeat 3x)*

And a ***Happy***   ***New***   ***Year***

Good   *tidings*   *we*   *bring*

To *you*   and   *your*   *kin*

Good   *tidings*   *for*   *Christmas*

And a *Happy*   *New*   *Year*
(Repeat)

"Filled-up Picnic Basket, A"

(Original Author Unknown, tune of "A Tisket, a Tasket", Illustrations
Copyright©2004 Time to Sign, Inc.)

A tisket, a tasket, a *filled-up picnic basket*.

Mom **stuffed** it with such *yummy* **treats**,

I **can't** **wait** to **unpack** it.

Unpack it, **unpack** it,

I   *can't*   *wait* to *unpack* it,

Crackers, cheese, and fresh *fruit*   *please*,

Kept *safe* tucked *in*   *our*   *basket*.

Our basket,   our basket,

There's ***more*** things ***in***   ***our***   ***basket***.

Juice and bars and ***my***   toy   ***cars***   to ***play*** with

– let's ***unpack*** it!

"Five Little Pumpkins"

(Original Author Unknown, tune of "Five Little Monkeys", Illustrations
Copyright©2004 Time to Sign, Inc.)

Five   *little*   *pumpkins* *sitting* on a *gate*,

Point to
thumb of "5"
handshape.

The *first*   one *said*, "Oh my it's getting *late*."

Point to index
finger of "5"
handshape.

The *second* one *said*, "There are *witches* in the *air*."

Point to middle finger of "5" handshape.

The *third* one *said,* *"We don't' care."*

Point to ring finger of "5" handshape.

The *fourth* one *said,* "Let's *run* and *run* and *run"*

Point to little finger of "5" handshape.

The *fifth* one *said,* *"I'm ready* for some *fun."*

Then "OOOH" went the *wind,*

And *OUT* went the *lights*,

And the *5*   *little*   *pumpkins*

rolled   *out* of *sight.*

"Jack-O'-Lantern"
(Original Author Unknown, tune of "I'm a Little Teapot", Illustrations
Copyright©2004 Time to Sign, Inc.)

I'm a **little jack-o'-lantern**   **fat** and **fine**

They **picked**   **me** off a **pumpkin vine**

Halloween is   **coming** don't **you**   **know**

Just **light**   **my candle**   and **watch   me glow**.

Time to Sign inc.

"Pumpkin, Pumpkin"

(Original Author Unknown, Illustrations Copyright©2004 Time to Sign, Inc.)

Pumpkin, pumpkin sitting   *on*   a   *wall,*

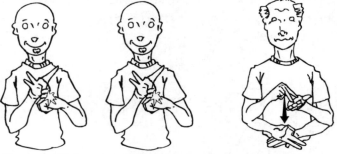

Pumpkin, pumpkin tip and *fall,*

pumpkin, pumpkin rolling down the *street*

Pumpkin, Pumpkin   trick or treat.

"Eight Little Candles"

(Original Author Unknown, tune of "Twinkle, Twinkle, Little Star", Illustrations
Copyright©2004 Time to Sign, Inc.)

Eight   *little*   *candles* in a *row*,

Waiting to *join* the   *holiday*   *glow*.

We will *light* them   *one by one*,

Until *all*   *eight* have *joined* the *fun*,

Eight   *little*   *candles* *burning*   *bright*,

Filling the *world* with *holiday*   *light.*

"I'm a Little Dreidel"

(Original Author Unknown, tune of "I'm a Little Teapot", Illustrations Copyright©2004 Time to Sign, Inc.)

I'm a   *little*   dreidel

I am a   *little*   *top*

When *you*   *twist*   *my*   *handle,*

I   spin   *until*   **I**   *drop!*

"Stars and Stripes"

(Original Author Unknown, tune of "Row, Row, Row Your Boat",
Illustrations Copyright©2004 Time to Sign, Inc.)

Wave, wave, wave the *flag*,

As *we* *march* around.

(hold flag up high)
Hold it high to *show* *our* *pride*,

It *must* not *touch* the *ground*. *(shake head)*

"Kwanzaa's Here"
(Original Author Unknown, tune of "Three Blind Mice", Illustrations
Copyright©2004 Time to Sign, Inc.)

Red,   green,   black,
Red,   green,   black.

Let's give a ***cheer, Kwanzaa's here.***

The ***decorations*** are ***quite***   a   ***sight,***

We   *light* a   *candle*   *every*   *night*,

The *holiday* is *filled*   with *light.*

Kwanzaa's   *here.*

CHAPTER 11:
LEARNING ASSIGNMENTS

Text Book Assignments for Chapters I – VIII

Chapter I: Benefits of Sign Language for Young Children.

1. In one paragraph explain when it is the best time for a child to begin learning sign language.

2. Write a one page essay on the benefits of teaching signing to hearing children.

3. In one paragraph detail how the use of sign language benefits teachers in the classroom.

4. Explain how you would incorporate the helpful hints and tips for teaching into your classroom instruction.

Chapter II: Early Childhood Social and Emotional Patterns of Development.

1. Write one page defining social and emotional development as it pertains to the education of young children.

2. Explain the similarities and differences between the Learning & Development Standards for 18-24 month old and three year old children.

3. Explain the differences between our logical and emotional brains.

4. Detail how the heart brain and gut brain can override the logical brain.

5. Describe which brain toddler and preschool age children spend most of their time utilizing, explain why this is the case, and detail how this effects their socialization with peers and learning.

6. Explain how social and emotional development affects academic learning and achievement.

7. Detail the six young children's social and emotional patterns.

Chapter III: Language and Communication Benchmarks.

1. Compare and contrast the language and Education Benchmarks for 18-24 month old and 3 year old children.

2. Explain the three channels of communication and provide an example of why voice itself does not always correctly convey meaning.

3. Specify why empathetic listening is important to the development of socialization skills and learning.

4. Explain when you should start signing with your children.

5. Detail how you would incorporate a learning topic (such as use of manners, positive expression of emotions, etc) into your daily routine with the children.

Chapter VI: Developmentally Appropriate Signs.

1. Compare and contrast two different age ranges communication developmental milestones. Detail the similarities and differences.

2. Demonstrate in class signs from two of the age groups.

3. Select a topic (use of manners, positive expression of emotions, etc.) and detail what activities you would use to teach your topic to either toddlers or preschool age children (your choice).

Chapter V: Activities & Signs to Enhance the Classroom & Behavioral Management.

1. List the activities you would incorporate into your everyday classroom routine.

2. In class demonstrate the classroom signs and sign phrases.

Chapter VI: Signing with Young Children with Special Needs.

1. List the special needs populations that typically use sign language and explain why they use it.

2. Describe the behavioral or other traits exhibited by special needs children that impact their learning.

3. Explain the social, emotional, and academic benefits for young special needs children.

4. Detail what you would suggest as the best way to begin signing with a young special needs child.

Chapter VII: Basic Signs for Young & Special Needs Children.

1. Be able to demonstrate your ability to reproduce these basic needs signs to the class.

Chapter VIII: Lessons & Themes.

Hint: Use the activities and handouts section to assist you with these assignments.

1. Master and demonstrate three sign language activities to teach young children (infants, toddlers, or preschoolers) their ABC's.

2. Master and demonstrate three sign language activities to teach young children (infants, toddlers, or preschoolers) manners.

3. Master and demonstrate three sign language activities to teach young children (infants, toddlers, or preschoolers) emotions.

4. Write a lesson plan to teach three topical areas using sign language activities. Explain after each area why you selected the activities you chose.

Resources

Federal Assistance and Support

Office of Child Care
U.S. Department of Health and Human Services
Administration for Children and Families
Office of Public Affairs
370 L'Enfant Promenade, S.W.
Washington, D.C. 20202
www.acf.hhs.gov/programs/occ

Corporation for National Service
Training and Technical Assistance
Room 4821
1201 New York Avenue, N.W.
Washington, D.C. 20595

Even Start
U.S. Department of Education
Compensatory Education Programs
Office of Elementary and Secondary Education
600 Independence Avenue, S.W.
Room 4400
Portals Building
Washington, D.C. 20202-6132
www.ed.gov/programs/evenstart

Office of Special Education Programs
U.S. Department of Education
600 Independence Avenue, S.W.
Switzer Building
Room 4613
Washington, D.C. 20202

Head Start
U.S. Department of Health and Human Services
Administration for Children and Families
Office of Public Affairs
370 L'Enfant Promenade, S.W.
Washington, D.C. 20202
www.acf.hhs.gov/programs

National Information Center for Children and Youth with Disabilities
P.O. Box 1492
Washington, D.C. 20013
www.icdri.org

National Institute of Child Health and Human Development
U.S. Department of Health and Human Services
National Institutes of Child Health
Building 31, Room 2A32, MSC-2425
31 Center Drive
Bethesda, MD 20842-2425
www.nichd.nih.gov

American Speech-Language-Hearing Association (ASHA)
10801 Rockville Pike
Rockville, MD 20852
301-897-700 (voice and TTY)
800-638-8255 (toll-free)
Website: http://www.cleft.com

Title I
U.S. Department of Education
Compensatory Education
programs
Office of Elementary and
Secondary Education
600 Independence Avenue, S.W.
Room 4400
Portals Building
Washington, D.C. 20202-6132

Organizations
Alliance for Technology Access
2175 East Francisco Boulevard
Suite L
San Rafael, CA 94901
415-455-4575

Gallaudet University
Washington, D.C.
(800) 526-9105

Other Resources
Dr. Marilyn Daniels
Associate Professor
Department of Speech Communication
Penn State University
120 Ridge View Drive
Dunmore, PA 18512-1699
Office 570 963-2670
FAX 570 963-2535
Mail to:mxd34@psu.edu

Council for Exceptional Children
(CEC)
Division for Children with
Communication Disorders
1920 Association Drive
Reston, VA 22091-1589
703-620-3660
Website: http://www.cec.sped.org

National Easter Seal Society
230 West Monroe Street
Suite 1800
Chicago, IL 60606-4802
312-726-6200
312-726-4258 (TTY)
Website: http://www.seals.com

Telephone Help

Child Care Aware
800-424-2246 (toll free)
Referrals to licenses and accredited childcare centers. Also provides a free packet of information on how to choose quality childcare. Coordinated by the National Association of Child Care Resource and Referral Agencies.

Weekdays, 9:00 a.m. – 5:00 p.m. (CST)

National Parent Information Network
800-583-4135
Referrals, abstracts, and answers from researchers free of charge

Weekdays, 8:00 a.m. – 4:30 p.m. (PST)

Single Parents Association
800-704-2102
Referrals to local support groups and community resources. Also, fields questions on parenting skills.

Weekdays, 9:00 a.m. – 6:00 p.m. (CST)

Websites

Time to Sign, Inc.
http://www.timetosign.com

NAEYC
http://www.naeyc.org

NHSA
http://wwww.nhsa.org

NIHSDA
http://www.nihsda.org

Websites (Continued)

Childbirth.Org
http://www.childbirth.org
Top discussion forums and a home page with answers to tough questions

Family.com
http://www.family.com
A Disney site. Bulletin board and chat rooms with voices of intelligent and caring parents.

http://www.geocities.com/babysigning
A guide for parents interested in signing with their babies.

http://www.aslpro.com

Dictionary lets users look up more than 2,800 signs, including common signs for babies.

http://www.masterstech-home/ASLDict.html
Has fewer signs that Handspeak.com but uses animation to help people learn signs.

Parent Talk Newsletter
http://www.tnpc.com/parentalk/index.html
Clearly written articles by physicians and psychologists.

Parenthood Web
http://parenthoodweb.com

Parenting Q&A
http://parenting-qa.com

Zero toThree
http://www.zerotothree.org

References

Chambers, Diane P. (1998). <u>Communicating in Sign: Creative Ways to Learn American Sign Language (ASL)</u>. New York: Fireside.

Daniels, Dr. Marilyn (2000). <u>Dancing with Words: Signing for Hearing Children's Literacy</u>. Westport, CT: Bergin & Garvey.

Hubler, Michael S. & Hubler, Lillian I. (2007). Classroom Management. Time to Sign, Inc., Indialantic, FL.

Hubler, Michael S. & Hubler, Lillian I. (2013). Everyone Can Sign: ADHD. Time to Sign, Inc., Indialantic, FL.

Hubler, Michael S. & Hubler, Lillian I. (2013). Everyone Can Sign: Autism. Time to Sign, Inc., Indialantic, FL.

Hubler, Michael S. & Hubler, Lillian I. (2013). Everyone Can Sign, Down Syndrome. Time to Sign, Inc., Indialantic, FL.

Hubler, Michael S. & Hubler, Lillian I. (2013). Everyone Can Sign: Infant-Toddler. Time to Sign, Inc., Indialantic, FL.

Hubler, Michael S. & Hubler, Lillian I. (2013). Lesson Planning Instruction Guide for Infant - Kindergarten. Time to Sign, Inc., Indialantic, FL.

Hubler, Michael S. & Hubler, Lillian I. (2001). The Learning Guide. Time to Sign, Inc., Indialantic, FL.

Hubler, Michael S. & Hubler, Lillian I. (2009). Young Children's Activity Guide. Time to Sign, Inc., Indialantic, FL.

Hubler, Michael S. & Hubler, Lillian I. (2008). Young Children's Themes Based Curriculum (Modules: Language Arts; Character; Community &

School; Foods, Farm, Garden & Animals; Family, Home, Holidays & Transportation; math, Science & Nature; Sports, Recreation & Arts; and Music). Time to Sign, Inc., Indialantic, FL.

References for Incorporating Signing into Your Daily Routine

Blanchard, Kenneth H. and Johnson, Spencer I (1981). The One Minute Manager. New York: Morrow.

Bonvillian, J. D., Orlansky, M. D., & Novack, L. L. (1983). Developmental milestones: Sign language acquisition and motor development. Child Development, 54, 1435- 1445.

Conflitti, C. (1998, February). Early Cognitive Development and American Sign Language. Exceptional Parent, 40-41.

Covey, Stephen R. (1989). The 7 habits of Highly Effective People. New York: Fireside.

Cutting, J. E. (1980). Sign Language and Spoken Language. Nature, 284, 661-662

Davis, L. (2000, January). Searching for sign, the language of home. The Chronicle of Higher Education, B4-B5.

Drasgow, E. (1998). American Sign Language as a Pathway to Linguistic Competence. Exceptional Children 64 (3), 329-342. Available at http://proquest.umi.com.

Felzer, L. (1998). A Multisensory Reading Program that Really Works. Teaching and Change, 5 (2), 169-183.

Hall, S. S. & Weatherly, K. S. (1989). Using Sign Language with Tracheotomized Infants and Children. <u>Pediatric Nursing, 15</u> (4), 362-367.

McCarthy, Kevin W. (1992). The On-Purpose Person. Colorado Springs: Pinon Press

Raimondo, B. (2000). Perspective. <u>Infants and Young Children, 12</u> (4), 4-7.

Senge, Peter M. (1999). The Fifth Discipline: the Art and Practice of the learning Organization. New York: Currency/Doubleday.

Signs of Success (1999). <u>Reading Today 16</u> (5), 14-15.

Time to Sign with Music Infant/Toddler Book and CD

16 Songs to Sign

- Animals on the Farm
- Apples and Bananas
- Bumble Bee
- Five Little Monkeys
- Happy Little Child
- If You're Happy and You Know It
- Itsy-Bitsy Spider
- Muffin Man
- Please and Thank You
- Row, Row Your Boat
- Six Little Ducks
- Ten Little Indians
- Three Little Monkeys
- Twinkle Little Star
- Where Are My Pets?
- Where is Thumbkin?

Time to Sign with Music Toddler/Preschool Book and CD

18 Songs to Sign

- ABC's (slow version)
- ABC's
- Bingo
- Buckle Bear Safety Song
- Car Song
- Down By the Station
- Fruit Song
- I'm a Firefighter
- I'm a Police Officer
- Make New Friends
- Mr. Sun
- Old McDonald Had A Farm
- Seven Days
- The Five Senses Song
- Veggies Song
- We've Been Playing
- Wheels on the Bus
- You Are My Sunshine

We See ... Stories

A fun and effective way to teach children colors and animals while going on an adventure. All signs are in English/Spanish/Sign.

5 Stories   *Farm Animals*   *Jungle Animals*

Ocean Animals   *Bugs*   *Pet Shop Animals*

Everyone Can Sign
Special Needs Series

 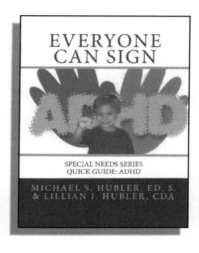 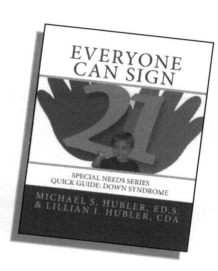

Autism   **ADHD**   **Down's Syndrome**

To order additional Time to Sign products please visit our web-site
www.TimeToSign.com
or call (321) 726-9466

To order additional Time to Sign products please visit our web-site www.TimeToSign.com or call (321) 726-9466

DR. MICHAEL & LILLIAN HUBLER

ABOUT THE AUTHORS

Dr. Michael and Lillian Hubler founded Time to Sign, Inc. in 2000. The company was founded because the Hublers recognized the benefits of using American Sign Language (ASL) with their children; and then to other children, families, educators, and care givers around the world. Time to Sign programs have been used in Family Childcares, Private Preschools, Early Head Start, Head Start, and School Districts.

Lillian is a nationally acclaimed presenter/trainer. Since 2000, she has trained over 50,000 educators, parents and children around the world in age appropriate and developmentally appropriate sign language usage. She is renowned for her high energy workshops and presentations. She has appeared on CNN, ABC, NBC, as we'll as interviewed by Florida Today and the Washington Post.

Michael is Director of Educational Curriculum and Product Development for Time to Sign. He is currently working on his doctorate dissertation in the field of education, specializing in the positive impacts of sign language on social and emotional development. Michael has served as an executive director for various educational and community services organizations for over 20 years, specializing in services and programs to enhance the education, personal growth, and development of at-risk children.

Michael and Lillian also owned a licensed day care with 135 children from birth to 12 years of age. They have written over 45 sign language books including preschool and school-age curriculums. Time to Sign's trainings and materials are uniquely designed to promote social emotional development and reduce children's challenging behavior in social settings. Their training programs and materials also promote literacy, language development, and communication.

Made in the USA
Middletown, DE
16 August 2024

59294770R00177